ACCELERANTS

ACCELERANTS

TWELVE STRATEGIES TO SELL FASTER, CLOSE DEALS FASTER, AND GROW YOUR BUSINESS FASTER

Michael A. Boylan

PORTFOLIO

PORTFOLIO
Published by the Penguin Group
Penguin Group (USA) Inc., 375 Hudson Street,
New York, New York 10014, U.S.A.
Penguin Group (Canada), 90 Eglinton Avenue East, Suite 700,
Toronto, Ontario, Canada M4P 2Y3
(a division of Pearson Penguin Canada Inc.)
Penguin Books Ltd, 80 Strand, London WC2R 0RL, England
Penguin Ireland, 25 St Stephen's Green, Dublin 2, Ireland
(a division of Penguin Books Ltd)
Penguin Books Australia Ltd, 250 Camberwell Road, Camberwell,
Victoria 3124, Australia
(a division of Pearson Australia Group Pty Ltd)
Penguin Books India Pvt Ltd, 11 Community Centre, Panchsheel Park,
New Delhi – 110 017, India
Penguin Group (NZ), Cnr Airborne and Rosedale Roads, Albany,
Auckland 1310, New Zealand
(a division of Pearson New Zealand Ltd)
Penguin Books (South Africa) (Pty) Ltd, 24 Sturdee Avenue,
Rosebank, Johannesburg 2196, South Africa

Penguin Books Ltd, Registered Offices:
80 Strand, London WC2R 0RL, England

First published in 2007 by Portfolio,
a member of Penguin Group (USA) Inc.

10 9 8 7 6 5 4 3 2 1

Copyright © Michael A. Boylan, 2007
All rights reserved

Illustrations by Jerry Begley

ISBN 978-1-59184-150-0

Printed in the United States of America
Set in Minion with Berthold Akzidenz Grotesk
Designed by Daniel Lagin

This book is dedicated to those people who model persistence in all its forms. Those who see the need to improve and have the foresight and confidence in themselves and the idea, such that they won't take no for an answer—pushing forward until they see their ideas in action. This is what I did in creating this material and process. It had to be out there in the world for all to use, because of its power and ability to genuinely benefit those who use it to achieve more of their dreams. Learn this process, use it respectfully, be a steward of the *ACCELERANTS,* and practice, practice, practice!

ACKNOWLEDGMENTS

I WOULD LIKE TO THANK THE FOLLOWING PEOPLE FOR THEIR GUIDANCE and feedback during the preparation and writing of this book. First, my thanks to Adrian Zackheim of Portfolio for his intuition and belief in how this material could benefit thousands of people and the organizations they work with. For his trust and confidence I am grateful.

I also wish to thank his very professional team: Adrienne Schultz, my editor; Will Weisser, associate publisher; and Shannon Garrison, my publicist, for their talent, dedication, and insight in making this a great book.

To my agent, Margret McBride, and her professional team who helped channel my energies during the writing of this book.

To our clients who have trusted this material enough to bring it into their organizations, shape it to their applications, and embrace it in the field as part of the way they go to market, driving more revenue performance and efficiencies to their organizations.

To some of my advisers and coaches who have helped guide me during the years in this business: Ken Blanchard, Larry Wilson, and

Harry Paul. To Bob Thele, former CEO of Covey Leadership; Mike Meyer, chairman of i360 Technologies and former CEO of Cap Gemini for the Americas; Jim Woodward, former head of Transformational Outsourcing for CGE&Y for the Americas; to John Murray, chairman of Advance Path and former CEO of PLATO Learning; Matt Shocklee, senior partner at PriceWaterhouseCoopers; Alain Thiry, president and CEO of EMSI and former president of The Carlson Marketing Group, Europe; Gary Gindele, former group vice president for Keane; and the many others who have advised me over the years.

To my family and friends for their support and encouragement along the way. And to Nancy Andzulis, Christine Krason, Mykael Sprague, Winnie Shows, Megan French, Vance Woolwine, John Bull, and Jerry Begly for all their help and expertise during the process. All together, a great team of professionals and trusted advisers for which I am grateful.

THE CORE BENEFITS OF THIS BOOK

*T*HIS BOOK WILL GIVE YOU AND YOUR PEOPLE BEST PRACTICE, FIELD-proven tools that can help everyone who impacts or generates revenue to drive more revenue to your business, more efficiently, and in less time.

I'll describe in detail twelve constraints that impede and sometimes block organizations from gaining more revenue, regardless of their size, allowing you to quickly diagnose which constraints are the biggest impediments to your companies' revenue growth, and take immediate action to minimize them.

The material goes even further by describing twelve field-proven tools called Accelerants. These tools can help minimize your constraints, helping you scope, sell, and close more and larger deals in less time, reducing your time-to-a-deal and cost of sales by as much as 25 percent. More specifically, these Accelerants will teach you how to:

- Target new revenue opportunities more efficiently and effectively
- Compress and make more efficient your existing sales process

- Craft stronger, more persuasive value propositions that create urgency to act

- Identify and gain access to the *real* decision makers faster and more effectively

- Condense and improve the power and delivery of your standard boilerplate presentations, delivering them in half the time you request

- More accurately assess and scope the likelihood of each opportunity's probability to close earlier in your courting process

- Increase the size of opportunities while weeding out those just kicking the tires

- Compress your closing cycles by up to 25 percent

- Reduce your cost of sales by up to 25 percent

- Energize your field force with tools they'll actually use because they work

- Foster empowerment, cohesion, and clarity of purpose within your organization.

That's what this material could do for you, your people, and your business! A tall order? You will be the judge of that. But based on the companies that have been using key Accelerants in their business for several years, some of which you'll read about shortly, you will soon see why these tools could also deliver for you.

The twelve Constraints and the twelve Accelerants are listed on two charts for your review on pages 6 and 7, so you can gain an immediate high-level overview of what they are. This will help you see quickly why the material is relevant, timely, and why it can directly impact your company's revenue performance and success going forward.

CONTENTS

Section One: The Constraints
*THE IMPEDIMENTS LIMITING THE SPEED AT WHICH YOU CAN
GROW YOUR BUSINESS*

Section Two: The Accelerant Principles
*TWELVE PROVEN PRINCIPLES TO OVERCOME, MINIMIZE, OR
DISSOLVE THE CONSTRAINTS TO YOUR BUSINESS'S GROWTH*

Section Three
THREE MORE ACCELERANT SUCCESS STORIES

Section Four
MOVING FORWARD

Section Five
WHERE TO TURN FOR ASSISTANCE

TWENTY YEARS OF SCULPTING

*T*HIS BOOK IS ABOUT IMPROVING YOUR ORGANIZATION'S TOP-LINE revenue performance and bottom-line profit by significantly shortening the sales and closing cycle(s) of your business. The Accelerants can make you and your people much more efficient and effective at targeting future business opportunities and shaping value propositions (at an enterprisewide or business unit level) that will resonate and cause urgency to act with the decision makers you want or need more access to. You can also gain access faster and more efficiently, with a presentation that will delight, essentially compressing your "time-to-a-deal."

This is new material, proven effective during the last eight years with several thousand professionals who have used it and experienced measurable productivity gains. The material has helped organizations increase their sales from both existing clients and prospects and even retrieve deals that were supposedly lost—driving greater market penetration and giving companies real competitive advantage in the marketplace.

These twelve field-tested tools and best practices are called

Accelerants because they can accelerate sales of more of your products, services, solutions, or concepts in less time, with less expense and effort. Each Accelerant principle is, in effect, a skill set and a mind-set—a plug-and-play solution representing a new, smarter, more aggressive, yet commonsense style of thinking about how and why this approach can help take your company to new heights. All twelve Accelerants offer companies either individual point solutions that can address specific areas of pain, and/or serve as a cohesive business development framework, improving the front end of your business hunting and gathering process.

Board members, CEOs and presidents, all levels of senior management, business owners as well as midlevel management, strategic growth and client-facing account managers, field-level marketing, sales and business development professionals will find real value in this material.

You may find it hard to believe that there's anything new to say or learn about the sales process. But the truth is that the sales, business development, and marketing methods of the past twenty years simply have not kept pace with the even greater complexities of doing business in a global economy. It's not because your current process doesn't work. It's that all the moving parts on the other side of your process, which are constantly in motion and ever changing, have gradually been eroding the effectiveness of your existing process. These include little things like:

- PROCUREMENT and PURCHASING procedures inside midsized and large companies that are radically changing the way your clients and prospects learn about your offerings. This changes the way you must approach and sell to these companies.

- The massive consolidation of DECISION-MAKING POWER and AUTHORITY into fewer people's hands, removing much of the decision-making autonomy from the individuals you typically work with and/or court on a day-to-day basis.

- The INCREASED LEVEL OF COMPETITION in your specific industry, which is putting more pressure on you to reduce your prices, add more value, and deliver even better customer service.

- The lack of what I call a COURTEOUS attention span on the part of some owners and many senior executives in large companies, who appear wired in meetings and unable to focus.

How do I know this? I have been a self-employed business owner and entrepreneur for twenty years, starting, growing, and eventually selling my ownership in two businesses, then beginning Accelerant International. I have a successful track record in targeting, getting in to meet with, presenting to, and closing the senior executive management of Fortune 1000 organizations and midsized entities in the United States, Canada, and abroad. Some of our clients include ADP, Microsoft's Certified Solution Providers, Research In Motion (maker of the BlackBerry), NCR, NEC Technologies, Ceridian, Mitel Networks, Logica/CMG, Cap Gemini Ernst & Young, PLATO Learning, Administaff, and others in the financial and professional services and different industry sectors.

The sales process is not rocket science, so what's the big deal? you may ask. Why venture out and consider something different, better, or more effective? Is it because your current process isn't working? Maybe. Is it because you're just tired of your process and want something new? Probably not. So why consider implementing certain Accelerants that could assist your current process, or even replace your entire process with the Accelerant Process for Business? Because these concepts can elevate your game and give you that unfair competitive advantage.

The Accelerant Process for Business helps the parent organization and respective business units align, refine, tighten, and metric their existing messages and value propositions to specific opportunities, targeted industry verticals, and audiences they serve. This process also assists the sales, marketing, business development, and strategic-planning organizations in becoming more proactive, efficient, and effective in driving more revenue and improving the margin on the business realized. Over time, the Accelerant Process could become as financially beneficial to your firm in the area of becoming more proficient and effective in growing your business as the Six Sigma process has, and continues to be for companies, in terms of helping improve several quality-related initiatives and processes.

Today, there are twelve common constraints that can and often do have a serious negative impact on most businesses. Some constraints are marketing related, some sales related. Others have to do with the marketplace and industry perceptions clients and prospects hold of your industry, the providers in it, and their views on your core offerings. Likewise, other constraints emanate from your own people's views and perceptions of the industry in which they do business, and of the offerings they represent to clients and prospects. The first section of this book describes these constraints in detail, explaining how and why they apply consistent downward pressure on your company, making you less efficient, effective, and profitable. These constraints can and do slow the growth of your business. Not every business faces all twelve, but most face at least four or five, and many face several. Typically, these constraints impact everyone in the organization, from the highest levels of senior management, to the marketing and customer service department, to the people in the field charged with bringing in and keeping business. After reading about the constraints, you will have a much better idea of those that are getting in your way.

Then I will present each Accelerant principle in the order in which they are designed to be used, providing the highest benefit for the user. Putting the Accelerant principles to work for you can help eliminate or overcome these constraints by blasting through them or dissolving them. You will learn what's behind each one, its specific value to your business, and how you can use them to garner more success.

Off-ramps throughout the material will lead you to additional information on certain Accelerants where training and back-end consulting will help tailor them to your specific applications, taking your business to that next level of sustained success.

Here is an overview of the twelve constraints and the twelve Accelerants:

THE CONSTRAINT CONTINUUM

There are several factors that negatively impact the performance
levels and overall effectiveness of any organization's business development efforts.
Below are the twelve constraints that can slow your business's growth.

THE TWELVE *ACCELERANT* PRINCIPLES

Individual skill sets you can use as plug-and-play point solutions in your existing business-development process as needed. Or taken as a cohesive framework that can be operationalized in the field, the *ACCELERANTS* offer companies an advanced business-development process that can be customized to each business unit to grow revenues from existing clients, targeted prospects, industry verticals, and stalled opportunities.

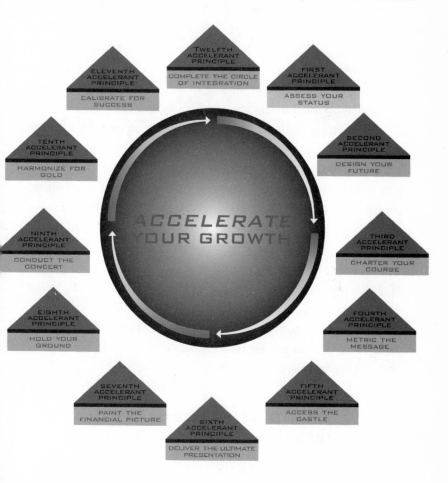

Using the Accelerants Process you and your business developers can get in faster to the right people and conduct more powerful meetings and calls once you are in. The meetings can also take less time than usual, to the delight of the people you are meeting with—and produce a better result.

Nobody can hide anymore. Growth systems need to be assessed in this more complex business environment in which all of us are playing to win. Your systems need to be assessed for whether they are capable of giving your company the tool sets to help you drive to new heights. You need tools and principles that will endure for the next twenty years. Accelerants can be those tools.

Your existing business hunting and gathering process may not need an overhaul. Or you may feel that just a few components are broken or need adjusting and that plugging a few Accelerants into your existing process might do the trick. Or after seeing how these principles complement one another, you may decide the entire Accelerant Process (customized to your business) might be the alternative you've been seeking. Use what you need and discard the rest. You get to be the judge and decide.

At the core of each Accelerant is a philosophy designed to garner a more respectful, courteous, productive, and efficient interaction between your company and all those with whom you choose to engage—so that all parties treat each other with a deeper level of grace and regard as business is transacted.

HOW THE ACCELERANTS AND THE ACCELERANT PROCESS FOR BUSINESS CAME INTO BEING: TWENTY YEARS OF SCULPTING

I am an entrepreneur. A partner and I spent seven years (1986–1992) building our first business—a North American distributorship for predictive dialing/call processing solutions. We sold these complex systems (hardware, software, and back-end support services) to Fortune 1000 corporations in the banking, credit card services, collections, and outbound telemarketing industries. Some of our competitors were sophisticated and well-funded giants like IBM-Rolm, AT&T, and Rockwell—great news for a couple of guys in their twenties with not a whole lot of experience.

Because we were selling to large, mostly publicly held corporations that were in no hurry whatsoever to buy and implement our smashingly fabulous, leading-edge technology, we had long selling cycles. Twelve to eighteen months seemed to be the norm, and sometimes it took two years. Because we started the business with a small loan, it was hardly "cush-city." We were nervous about where the next deal would come from and when. And because this was our first run at being entrepreneurs, it was a bit like "the blind leading the blind." The average purchase price for our offerings was about $79,000 per five-station system, with some clients purchasing ten, twenty, and in a few cases, one hundred-plus stations. We had big dreams, a short rope, and we needed to eat. I was the one charged with "getting in the door fast" with these large corporations to someone who, we hoped, had the authority to make the decision.

To shorten our closing cycles we tried to get into an organization as high as possible for the initial meeting. I was focused on presenting our wares to senior executives, not the mid- and lower-level managers who would say nice things, recommend another meeting, and gladly accept our typical follow-up in the form of an expensive meal. We didn't have the funding to wait around forever, attend another meeting or two, or twelve, before determining if we had a live one or not. Because we didn't have the staying power of our competitors, I had to figure out how to close business opportunities smarter and faster than they did. This meant creating access at a relatively high level (not necessarily in the IT department), sometimes to multiple senior executives all at once, as fast as humanly possible, so we could tell our story and assess the landscape. Then, if there was real interest, we could drive things from the top down, versus the classic bottom up.

The result was a methodology I developed through years of experimentation and use, now called the Circle of Leverage System or COL—a process that now possesses several U.S. trademarks and is one of the reasons for our success. The COL System resulted in signed contracts with Fingerhut, Household International, Citigroup in the United States and Europe, Payco American (the largest third-party collection agency in the nation at that time), I.C. System, Harris Bank, Time-Life, and many other corporations of this size and scope—to the surprise and irritation of our huge competitors.

The COL System (see the fifth Accelerant) was very effective at increasing our hit rate for first meetings at a high level within large and midsized organizations that had no urgency to buy, were not even looking for a solution, and could be most difficult to gain entry into, let alone at the highest levels.

Securing one or two senior-level executives in these "first meetings" inside large corporations was a pleasing and frequent result of the COL System. But this type of audience in first meetings and in subsequent meetings forced us into a very different kind of conversation—and a different kind of presentation. These high-level executives had far less time on their hands, were sometimes less cordial, and had more pressure to deal with. They weren't at all interested in *the chat,* having a robust conversation, or having the consultative approach used on them. Many didn't seem to care for our artfully coifed questions, designed to get them to open up about the business challenges and pains they needed to address. These were brilliant questions like, *"Tell me Steve . . . what keeps you up at night?"* This approach actually seemed to bother them, even though this was how I was trained as a salesperson. This was supposed to be the appropriate way to approach all potential business opportunities. In fact, many sales and management training companies throughout the country still teach this approach today.

These executives, however, wanted (and expected) me to get to the point—the financial point, the teeth, as they would bark—as quickly as possible. Within the first few minutes of the meeting, as we were about to fire up the thirty-plus slide deck of our beautiful and well-thought-out PowerPoint presentation to tell them who we were, what we did, who we've helped (which was basically nobody in the early years), they would bark out things like:

"You know what, Michael, before we begin here, how can you help us? I mean, at the end of the day, what's the 'net-net' here? Give us some meat. Give us some TEETH. How can you people really help us?"

I wasn't prepared. I was fast on my feet, but to be frank, I didn't know how to answer to their satisfaction or with any level of specificity or clarity. I thought my job was to learn where their business challenges and pains were coming from by asking the right consultative questions, but this approach caused many of these meetings to hit a brick wall. They came to an end faster than I could blink, without understanding what had just happened. After all that great work to get in so high with these companies, we lost the opportunity because we didn't deliver our message the way the executives wanted to hear it.

This level of pain and failure caused me to eventually figure out, and then create, another process . . . another tool set. I developed a methodology to grind down the messages and value propositions (which providers usually think are fine and totally clear already). I also figured out how to articulate in the first couple minutes of any meeting, conference call, or web-x demo—the financial TEETH—the "net-net," as these high-level types liked to say—that our offerings could deliver. This change in our approach has become the fourth Accelerant, METRIC THE MESSAGE, which you will learn about shortly. I began using both these methodologies in our businesses with great results. But there was even more these high-level executives and owners expected in the early meetings to help them separate the wheat from the chaff. They were not willing to sit through, or even look at, our gorgeous PowerPoint presentation. They expected me to share the TEETH of our solution—low side, high side—in these first meetings and to compress my entire pitch by at least half. They wanted "the meat," as they would call it, right away, literally within the first five minutes of the meeting or call—not the typical way, buried somewhere toward the end.

I eventually learned they'd use this information to determine if they were impressed enough to stay in the meeting. If not, the key person or people in the room would basically leave, saying something like:

"Michael, I'm glad you've come to us today with your solution. Clearly, there could be some application here for our organization, and I'll leave that to the capable people who are in this room with you now. I have the utmost trust and confidence in them, and therefore, I will leave it to them to tell me how we should proceed from here, and whether it would be prudent at this time to really dig in and take a hard look at what you have by doing some type of RFP (request for proposal). I apologize, but I need to step out and attend to some other matters. But please, keep going with your presentation, and we will be in touch, OK?"

They said this in the softest, most persuasive of tones, like warm butter on lobster, with that puppy-dog look of utter genuineness on their faces. I of course, thought, "Great. We have his or her buy-in so far, so let's keep going." How stupid I was—because what I eventually came to learn was, the meeting was *over*. Not just, maybe we had a chance down the road—the meeting was *done*. I had *lost* my window with the top person or people who were the primary decision maker(s) in large corporations, where nobody makes any big decisions without several key people signing off.

I was angry, irritated, and determined to overcome this recurring frustration with large and midsized corporations. Eventually, I learned that owners of small businesses process information and want it delivered to them in the same way. They want the bottom line, and they want it up front. I dramatically modified our presentation style to do exactly that, developing another process—now a best practice called the 1/3rd . . . 2/3rds Condensed Presentation Format, and part of the sixth Accelerant, DELIVER THE ULTIMATE PRESENTATION.

So over the course of several years of experimentation and development on large and midsized organizations, I had become highly proficient at:

1. Getting in as high as possible, as fast as possible, to one or more real decision makers.

2. Articulating a crisper, more financially oriented value proposition to senior-level people.

3. Presenting in a greatly compressed time span, where "the meat" was presented right away and the entire presentation was finished in one-third the time I had requested, to the surprise and delight of those in the meetings.

These three methodologies were a radical departure from the way our large competitors were selling. Those companies had billions in revenues, plenty of cash, and expense accounts dedicated to allowing their salespeople to build that relationship by using the classically accepted consultative approach to selling. Meaning they had the time and the luxury of a big company image behind them, to ask the kinds of questions such as "What keeps you up at night?" or "What areas of your business are you experiencing the greatest challenges with?", etc. Don't get me wrong. The consultative approach works. I use it too, and it is certainly one effective way of going about selling whatever it is you have to sell. However, it is only one way.

The large companies we were competing against had staying power—while we did not. I needed to know as fast as humanly possible from every company we met with: *Are you guys really interested or not? And if so, who should be in meetings two and three so that we can move the ball forward?*

I refined these three methodologies during the early years through consistent use on different-size companies, tailoring them around a variety of scenarios and applications we encountered. They worked with clients we were trying to grow as well as with prospects, new vertical industry sectors, and opportunities we had recently lost to a competitor. In fact, you'll read about a scenario with Household International where that was the case. These tools were also helpful when companies we had been meeting with suddenly stopped returning our phone calls. As an entrepreneur, this would drive me nuts, so I tailored ways to use the principles in these situations as well. I was constantly tweaking them to help us in the myriad situations one encounters in a life of sales and influencing others. Becoming one of the industry's major players was proof for me that these battle-tested methodologies were producing good results—we had the revenues to prove it.

I used these tools to launch a second company with my partner and another friend. Verifications, Inc., is a provider of background credential verification to the human resource departments of Fortune 1000 corporations. I was about to see if these tools worked in another industry where I had no experience, no credentials, no track record, no referrals or ways to get in the door—just as I had entered the technology industry. I am pleased that Verifications, Inc., remains one of the preeminent providers of these services throughout the Midwest.

Feeling confident on the heels of two successes and armed with three strategic weapons that proved effective over several years of use on large and midsized organizations, fast forward to the period 1992 through 1994, when I took a flyer. Selling my ownership in the first two companies, I turned to the music industry with the intent of getting a recording contract as a singer with a major record label—a dream since my teenage years.

Things got interesting when, after spending several hundred thousand dollars in the recording studio, my three field-tested methodologies landed me conference calls and in-person meetings with CEOs and SVPs of A&R (the top person in charge of talent acquisition) of the largest record labels, many of whom were multibillion-dollar music and entertainment conglomerates.

None of the executives felt the music I had recorded was worthy of a recording contract, yet they were peppering me with questions about how I was getting meetings and conference calls with such high-level people in the business without any referrals, credentials, or experience in the industry I wanted to become a part of.

These music executives would interrupt my pitch within minutes with questions like:

"Michael, hold on for a minute. Is it correct that you've also had some meeting or call a week or two ago with my peer over at RCA? And you've also spoken with the SVP of A and R at Arista Records? Is this correct?"

As soon as I'd acknowledge that it was true, they'd jump in with:

"Son, how are you doing this? It appears you are using some type of pattern on all of us, aren't you?"

"Yes, sir, I am," I would say.

"And what is it that you are doing? Do you know what you are doing to get these meetings with people like me? I mean, do you know what it is that I do here? I run this label basically. How is it that you are able to get us to pay attention to you, without any experience in this business? Don't you think it's just a tad unusual for you to be talking with those of us who run these multibillion-dollar organizations? I think it's amazing. I am not interested in your music, to be very frank. But what I might be interested in learning more about is how you might help our sales organization do whatever it is you are doing on the people that we want to approach."

This was not what I wanted to hear, but this same response from several big labels led to something else. My music career had officially come and gone, but I now had the impetus for Accelerant, and the creation and build-out of additional Accelerant principles into one cohesive and powerful framework for the front end of a company's business development efforts.

WHY THE ACCELERANTS AND THE ACCELERANT PROCESS FOR BUSINESS WILL BECOME YOUR NEW BEST FRIENDS

What you will learn has been battle tested in the field by me and by thousands of others. You *must* take a close look at the process you are using to target, hunt, qualify, and close business. Identify those areas that could be lacking and weak, so they can be improved and enhanced. You want your business to remain strong and even prosper in the wake of constant market turbulence, which is becoming the norm. The Accelerants and the Accelerant Process for Business can do exactly that. This is a set of repeatable field-proven principles and a process that can deliver amazing results, while allowing you to flex the process so it can be tailored to numerous selling, marketing, and growth-oriented situations.

In recent years, large and midsized companies have not invested much in their people in terms of sales, business development, and management training. In fact, senior management has often ignored this area because it's an easy target to justify cutting. The result has been companies that have become rusty, complacent, and out of touch with how inefficient their standard sales and marketing approaches have become.

Many sales processes don't work anymore—period. But companies don't know exactly what's not working, or why, or what needs fixing. What's worse, many companies are in denial that their processes are broken and will not support what they need to do going forward. The Accelerants can address the impediments to growth going on within thousands of companies, between buyers and sellers, and the marketplace forces, which are constantly changing.

Take heart in the advice and feedback scores of clients have provided to help me create a set of Accelerants that can serve as your new cohesive front-end business framework for targeting, hunting, and gathering more business for the next twenty years. Being a student of this material, as I have been as its creator, I know you will learn how the tools work and how they can serve the highest and best use within your organization for a long time to come.

Section One: The Constraints

THE IMPEDIMENTS LIMITING THE SPEED AT WHICH YOU CAN GROW YOUR BUSINESS

THE CLIENT OR PROSPECT'S GENERAL PERCEPTIONS OF YOUR INDUSTRY

*T*HE FIRST CONSTRAINT IS A SUBTLE ONE. CLIENTS AND PROSPECTS will rarely talk about it because it telegraphs their negotiating strategy and, understandably, they don't want to lose any leverage when it comes time to negotiate for the best price, service, and support.

The way a client or prospect perceives companies in your sector can tell you a great deal about what they will expect from your company and how they will behave as an organization during the courting process, up to the point of a signed agreement and beyond. Their perspective also influences how they will treat you as a vendor/provider during your business relationship. Not knowing how they perceive companies in your general industry can leave you with a blindfold on, merely guessing as to how they will respond at every step of the courting process.

I was pursuing a services firm that provided a comprehensive suite of offerings to large and midsized organizations across numerous industry verticals. The firm, a division of a multibillion-dollar conglomerate, was taking a hard look at our company and a few others.

They wanted to help several hundred senior producers engage at a higher level, with a tighter, financially oriented value proposition and presentation for use in the first few senior-level meetings. Their goal was to drive more closed deals in a compressed time horizon. The opportunity represented a nice slice of business for us, so we were diligent in courting their vice president of business development.

He scheduled several conference calls and then missed them, routinely did not return our calls, and dragged his decision out several months longer than he indicated he could. He verbally awarded us the business, asked us to send the contract for review and signature, but never returned calls once he had it. All the while, he hid behind his executive assistant, who by then was beside herself, apologizing for his behavior. To top it off, he never signed our deal, never went with anyone else, and never told us the real reason why. It was clear through his cavalier attitude and unprofessional actions that he viewed us, our service offerings, and the others he was considering as peons who were ready to jump at a moment's notice when he said "Jump." This sort of treatment is hardly enjoyable; in fact, it can make you feel cranky and downright powerless when you're in the throws of it all.

When potential buyers perceive all providers in an industry as basically the same, they can sometimes behave this way. Regardless of your company's size and market dominance, you are not immune to this perception, and you can't control it. Potential buyers will either have it or they won't.

Perceptions are extremely powerful, not to mention hard to change. If the prospect's view at the outset is "The top five companies are all pretty close—if one company has certain traits, the others probably do too," this would be beneficial to know as early as possible in your courting process. For example, when a large firm is considering outsourcing its IT operations and wants to engage with some of the largest providers who offer these types of services, they'd probably contact IBM, EDS, CSC, Keane, Accenture, and other offshore firms such as Wipro, Tata, etc. Often, senior executives are the ones who will make the decision, and sometimes will view the offerings of all these providers as vanilla—each company essentially interchangeable with all of their competitors. This is what can foster the attitude of indifference or arrogance. Next, they schedule (through procurement) a bakeoff among the top vendors, because they feel it is so difficult to decipher any real difference among the available options.

The prospect or client's specific perceptions can be a constraint that will impede the pace at which you bring in business, and at what margin. They link two crucial elements: their current perceptions of your industry and the providers in it, and the behavior they think they can get by with when negotiating the deal. If competition is quite fierce among the top vendor/providers in a market, educated organizations may take advantage of the situation. If they believe a particular industry or product is not that complex, or that they can source the product or service without much extra hassle—be careful, because they may try.

One of my peers owns a successful women's handbag manufacturer. One of their largest customers is the second largest retailer in their segment in the nation. It is amazing to me that he continues to work with that level of pressure from this retailer's central purchasing and procurement department. They told him he could have the business for another "x" years—but more than likely, after that period, he would have to bid against them because they would become a competitor. In point of fact, he had been such a good business partner by teaching them the ins and outs of his business, the retailer decided to enter that industry themselves by private labeling their own women's handbags. In effect, everything he had done to foster the relationship over the years would be used against him. My guess is that, within a period of time, he will either lose the business or decide it is no longer worth the time and angst. You can see a situation like this coming, and one of the key reasons is the client's general view of your industry.

In my friend's case, by being so helpful to his client, he has inadvertently helped the retailer learn so much about his business that it validated the retailer's perceptions of his industry, and proved their theory that they didn't need him. In the end, he may lose his largest client by being so helpful and cooperative as a vendor-supplier.

So much for their comments regarding wanting a long-term, strategic relationship with their vendors. There may be no love in Muddsville if they feel they can get into your business that easily. Understandably, because of the uncertainty that can exist over the course of a relationship, most buyers want maximum long-term leverage and control over the duration, nature, and quality of their relationships with vendor-providers. Their knowledge and deep-seated beliefs and perceptions about your industry can cause serious hiccups to your cash flow. And this will impede your growth.

Your efforts to overcome their perceptions with added focus on finding that competitive advantage or most compelling key differentiators become all the more critical. The example I chuckle about is when organizations implore their sales, marketing, and business development executives to focus on "the value add" they bring to the party. However, the organizations you deal with can and sometimes do see right through this dog and pony show. In my experience, when they have given vendor-providers the benefit of the doubt and allowed them to substantiate their claims of value add, many haven't been able to do so with any level of believability. And this reinforces the prospect's initial perceptions, which are now on the way to becoming cement.

There's an amazing dynamic that takes place when one company begins courting another—especially when the company doing the courting is one of the top players in their particular industry. The level of trust shown toward the provider will vary according to the level of executive in the prospect or client organization being courted.

I have developed a valuable tool called the Trust Continuum that helps predict how your clients and prospects will perceive your industry, as well as your offerings. You can then anticipate how they may behave. The Trust Continuum describes how different individuals may respond and feel about the top-tier companies in a particular industry that are courting their business. It will help you better understand from their vantage point how potential buyers are likely to perceive and react to vendors as a function of the specific levels of power, authority, and titles they hold within their own firm.

The big secret is this: The most significant influences impacting how they may behave with providers are the title and level of power and authority the prospect or client holds within their firm. Generally speaking, the more power and authority a person has, the less favorably they perceive the top players courting their business. How does this help you? For one thing, it can save your company time, hassle, and above all valuable resources. This information also helps you and your people be smarter about tailoring your approach to the companies you want to target.

Years ago when I began my sales career, our clients often used the expression "Nobody ever got fired for going with IBM." I used to think about that a lot, feeling it was probably true to a large extent, even though it would be impossible to prove. But it just seemed true, because IBM was, and still is, so large and powerful. The real premise behind that statement is that rarely does anyone ever get fired for selecting a top provider. As a result, companies throughout the world strive to own a top spot in the minds of clients and prospects by becoming one of the premier three to five leading providers in their particular industry.

I've discovered that people in middle and lower levels of management and below frequently tend to place more reverence, trust, respect, and overall comfort in the top three to five providers in any particular industry. Why? Because, truth be told, selecting a "top provider" acts as a safety net or security blanket in holding on to their jobs. It helps justify their decisions. However, beginning with vice presidents and above, the reverse begins to be true. In many cases, the higher the title, level of power, and authority to spend money, the less trust and reverence they have for the top providers.

Why is this? It is because top executives on the buying side understand the concepts behind raw leverage and how to use it. It's not a secret to them. They are hip to how large providers will use their muscle and market-leading leverage to gently persuade buyers, driving the size, scope, and duration of the deals. And they know who within their own organization are most persuaded by the large providers.

Higher-level execs know all too well that engaging with one of the top providers is sometimes like dancing with the devil. Once you enter into the relationship, it can be difficult to unwind because of the sheer size and power of the provider. As a result, senior execs believe that one of the attributes of a successful vendor/client relationship is maintaining some element of control and leverage over the provider. Maintaining some level of command and control over a top provider in any industry niche—especially companies the size and scope of an IBM—can be tricky. In the event that something goes wrong in the relationship, senior executives know how challenging it can be to get the vendor's attention to rectify the problem. They believe that, at the end of the day, "It's all about leverage. They either need us or they don't." And in business it's good to be needed, because if you're not, good luck getting anybody's attention.

This ingrained belief plays itself out in how they will shop you for the best deal and negotiate with you—all to make sure they do their best to ensure, via the terms and conditions of the contract, that they will be taken care of. And if not, there are clear remedies they can take to put sufficient leverage on the provider to get things resolved. At the end of the day, it's all about trust. The Trust Continuum depicts this dynamic to help you shape your strategy for approaching people in prospect and client organizations.

In addition to using the Trust Continuum, I have developed the following questions that allow you to go to the source to better understand this first constraint. You can learn your clients' and prospects' perceptions of your industry by drawing them into a dialogue with some carefully worded questions such as these:

Q1. What are your perceptions of the companies that offer products, services, and solutions in this industry?

Q2. Could your current perception of providers in this sector change? If so, what would these companies need to do to change it?

Q3. Is there anything that irritates you that companies in this industry do? Anything they would need to change for your perception to change?

Q4. What elements within your current provider's business development, sales, or business-gathering process should improve? How should they be improved?

Q5. How many other companies are you aware of that could supply a similar set of products, services, or solutions at a price comparable

THE TRUST CONTINUUM

The higher the title, the less reverence, trust, and regard executives can have when dealing with an industry leader, resulting in more emphasis on the terms and conditions of the contract.

Chairman/CEO

President/COO/CFO/CIO

Executive VP/Business Unit Heads

Senior Vice Presidents

Group/Area Vice Presidents

Vice Presidents

Assistant Vice Presidents

Directors/Area General Managers

Managers/Supervisors/Field Leaders

**Assistant Managers/Assistant Supervisors/
Task Force Leaders**

Titles below the vice-president level frequently place more reverence, trust, and regard in courting vendor-providers who are industry leaders. They feel it can help them make safer decisions, help justify their decisions, and hold on to their jobs.

to your current provider? Please provide the names of these organizations.

Q6. Are there any significant benefits your current vendor provides that you believe you could not attain from another? If so, what are those benefits?

Remember, the answers to these questions can differ based on the title of the person giving their opinions. Therefore, you might want to ask these questions numerous times of various levels of people within the organization to help gain a deeper perspective of how levels of executives up and down the target organizations view your industry.

Here is a second version of these questions, which you should ask the people in your own organization. Their answers will help provide a valuable path of information specific to internal impediments to getting more business. Pose these Constraint Assessment questions to your employees, agents, distributors, and independent contractors:

Q1. How do you feel clients and prospects view our company and other providers in our general industry? Please be specific.

Q2. Why do you feel they view our organization and perhaps others in our industry in this way?

Q3. Is the perception you have described changeable? If not, why?

Q4. If you were running our company, what elements and/or processes would you change that might positively enhance the way clients and prospects view our company?

Q5. Which elements, situations, or events are negatively impacting how clients and prospects view our company?

Q6. Which aspects about our company are you fairly certain existing clients and prospects don't like?

Q7. What would need to happen for these perceptions to change?

If you ask these questions in the right environment and remain open to the feedback, this exercise can help paint a picture as to whether this first constraint is an impediment to the growth of your business. These questions are part of a larger assessment tool that you can find at www.accelerantinternational.com.

THE CLIENT OR PROSPECT'S PERCEPTION OF YOUR CORE OFFERINGS—OR THEIR CURRENT PROVIDER'S SOLUTION

*T*HINK ABOUT IT. IF YOU ARE ALREADY IN A RELATIONSHIP WITH THE client, they have seen you naked. They have negotiated with you before (and perhaps simultaneously with your key competitors—to keep you in check, of course). They have met with you several times and now have some level of experience with your people and the products, services, or solutions they are currently buying. They *know* whether you've performed against initial perceptions and expectations—both theirs and their corporation's.

They have experienced you and your company at your best and perhaps even at your worst. They have noticed if you arrive at meetings less prepared than before your relationship was in place, and they have experienced your products or services in a live environment. They may have been delighted to discover that what they are purchasing has performed above their level of expectation. In any case, they have an even deeper set of firsthand evidence to reinforce or revamp their initial perceptions.

This constraint emerges at the front end of your new business-gathering process. Now that the customer has already purchased, implemented, and experienced your products, services, and solutions, they have a basis—a platform—on which to judge them. If initial performance is not at least at par in their eyes, this constraint can become an obstacle in contract negotiations down the road, because they will have even more leverage.

As a case in point, look at the pressure the advertising industry worldwide has been under, as evidenced by megamergers and giant acquisitions by mega agencies such as Omnicom, WPP, Interpublic, Publicis Groupe Worldwide, and Dentsu. One of the primary drivers fueling this level of merger mania is—guess what—the lack of satisfaction clients are feeling about the results they are getting for their money. This is not the answer you'll get from the agencies, of course. Their spin is that they are doing this to provide better economies of scale for their clients, allowing their dollars to go even further. I'm sure there is also some truth in that. But the industry acknowledges that the market pressures and the dynamics of the business make it harder and harder to drive and deliver the kinds of responses to campaigns that clients demand.

Every once in a while, you can read in the *Wall Street Journal* about certain large corporations that have put their advertising business "up for review." This lingo is ad speak for "We are questioning the results we've been getting to date and are going to look at other options to make sure we are getting the best results possible for the dollars we're putting out."

If the prospect is purchasing a competitive product, service, or solution but has yet to engage with your company, their set of experiences with the competitive offering will most definitely affect your courting and negotiation process in some form or fashion. So will the perceptions they have already created from seeing your competition naked.

To assess whether this second constraint is impeding your growth, here are some pointed questions from the Constraints Assessment to ask clients, prospects, and your own people.

Ask your clients and prospects:

Q1. In your opinion, what makes our products, services, or solutions special or unique? Do they provide specific competitive advantages? If so, what are they?

Q2. How would changing vendors/providers affect your business? Would there be any measurable impact? If so, please describe. If there would be little or no impact, please explain why.

Q3. Do you recall what made your company choose our company as your current provider/supplier? If so, what were those key elements, factors, or capabilities?

Q4. How would you rate our company on a scale of one to ten, with one being poor, five average, and ten exceptional?

Here are key assessment questions you can ask your people, independent agents, distributors, and other entities that assist you in marketing your products and services. Their feedback will help determine if this second constraint could be negatively impacting your growth.

Q1. How do you think current clients and prospects view our core offerings, products, and services in relation to other potential providers? Please be specific.

Q2. Why do you think they have this perception?

Q3. Could anything affect or change this perception? If so, what would that be?

Q4. What do you think has been the biggest roadblock to our business development and acquisition process, related to how clients and prospects perceive our products, services, and core offerings?

Q5. Can these elements or impediments be changed? If so, how?

YOUR TEAM'S PERCEPTION OF YOUR BUSINESS, PRODUCTS, AND SERVICES

*H*AVE YOU EVER HEARD ONE OF YOUR PEERS MAKE A DEROGATORY COM- ment about your company's products or services? Maybe it was just a minor "slam," indicating their discontent or lack of belief in them. I can assure you, as one who has dealt with and trained thousands of seasoned, high-level sales producers, client account managers, marketing executives, and senior management, I hear it a good bit—at sales meetings, annual conventions, and in the halls during breaks. Let me pose a question: What percentage of your sales, business development and marketing force, client-facing customer service, and account relationship managers actually believe in the value that your products, services, and/or solutions deliver for your clients?

It's a hard question to answer, isn't it? Would you say it's 100 percent? I bet not. Maybe 95 percent? Less than 90 percent? Those who are not fully on board with a rock-solid belief in the benefits of your offerings have a negative impact on achieving growth and revenue targets for the company. They may be acting like a slow-growing cancer within your firm, constraining your efforts and the company's revenue targets.

I am not overdramatizing the situation. In fact, let's just run the numbers to see what type of impact a fair-weather business developer can have on your business. Think of the producers we call "fence-sitters"—individuals who can just as easily bash or make fun of your company's offerings as say good things about them. The question really should be "How good do you think these people are at acting?" They may believe they are faking out your clients, but more likely, clients are picking up on your people's real beliefs about the products and services they represent.

Let's do an exercise to see what type of financial impact this lack of a positive perception can potentially have on the organization. For the sake of this example, let's assume 10 percent of your business developers are not convinced about the value of the offerings they represent. And let's say your nationwide sales force is a hundred individuals strong. In this case, that leaves ten people who are not 100 percent on board and probably not pushing as hard as the other ninety producers—ten fence-sitters.

Let's also assume that everyone has an annual sales quota of one million dollars in closed business, and that it's imperative the company achieve one hundred million in revenues—which, by the way, the CEO has committed to Wall Street by telling two high-profile analysts who cover your company's stock performance. So Wall Street and the investment community are watching.

Ninety individuals nail their number, giving you ninety million in revenue. But you need one hundred million, because that's what was committed to Wall Street. So let's look at what the fair-weather fence-sitters have produced—the ones you heard make a couple of not-so-casual slams on your company's offerings at the last sales conference. Not surprisingly, they each came in at around 50 percent of quota at best, with a list of excuses a mile long as to why they missed it: The quota was just too high; the pricing of the product or service is out of kilter with the rest of the market competitors; there was a huge snowstorm on the East Coast that shut down all the airports, preventing them from getting face to face with the customer to ink the deal; or their mother or father fell ill and needed their time and attention. Heard any of this before? In fact, these individuals are so convincing about why they missed their number, you only wish they'd used that same level of energy to close more business.

Now you are five million short for the year . . . ninety-five million versus the hundred million you committed to Wall Street. No problem, you think to yourself. That's not that bad . . . you're only 5 percent off the target. So Wall Street is going to ding your stock accordingly by 5 percent, right? Wrong—totally wrong. How about five times that number? The company will lose millions in market value, and you, all the employees who own stock in the company, *and* your shareholders are now going to be the recipients of a 20 to 30 percent drop in the value in your holdings.

And why did this happen, you ask yourself, with an expression that looks as though you could spit nails? Well, it was primarily the result of ten fence-sitters who thought nothing of making a few subtle, degrading comments about your offerings. You perhaps laughed it off at the time as no big deal. But now you're not laughing. Instead, you feel like showing these people the door. Their attitude just cost you big time. This situation does happen in companies, but often the damage has already been done, and all that can be done is to make sure it doesn't happen in the future.

As you can see, this third constraint can be dangerous to your company if you don't nip it in the bud, and quickly. So if you'd like your company to be free of cancerous attitudes, understand what everyone who contributes revenue to the business perceives and believes about the value your products, services, and solutions deliver for clients.

There has been a great deal written about belief systems and their power to affect outcomes. But not everyone openly shares their beliefs and perceptions about your company and its offerings. Now add to the mix these key global business trends:

- massive consolidation

- price pressure

- margin erosion

- increased corporate fraud and litigation

- a greater attitude of entitlement in some senior management

- far less camaraderie and loyalty among "the doers" and management

Several of these patterns are due to consolidation across industries, and all of these affect multiple industry sectors. These trends are not going away anytime soon, and they may become more widespread. As a result, more and more employees throughout the world—even in management—have become more nervous about job security. So they keep many of their deep-seated perceptions about their company and its product and service offerings to themselves, lest an unpopular comment come back to haunt them.

At the end of the day, however, the perceptions of your employees can be a significant constraint that directly impacts your company's financial performance. Every single producer has observations and opinions about your company and its products, services, solutions, and causes, which can and often do affect your company's revenue line.

The perspective of your front line—the sales and business development, marketing, customer service, and customer-facing consultants, managers, client executives, independent agents, and distributors—are especially crucial. Their perceptions of the intrinsic value your offerings bring to another company and their customers absolutely affect several factors—minor things like their overall attitude toward clients and coworkers, their level of effort, and desire to perform. This affects all performance levels—how frequently they utilize their health-care benefits, their willingness to be on time, etc.

As a preventive measure against a sudden decline in your revenue line, ask your front line some questions in a safe, nonthreatening environment. This is often the only way of getting candid responses to employees' deeply held beliefs about the organization and its offerings. This valuable data can telegraph problem areas before they become major issues—allowing you time to deal with them head on.

We suggest asking the following questions of anyone and everyone involved in a customer-facing role inside your company to see if this third constraint could be impeding your growth and strategic planning efforts. Here are a few of the Constraint Assessment questions we use with clients—who ask their people the following questions:

Q1. How would you rate or rank our core offerings in relation to other directly competitive offerings?

Q2. Do you feel our current offerings provide any compelling benefits that help you legitimately differentiate, posture, or close business opportunities when positioned against substantial competitors? Please list them in the order from most to least compelling.

Q3. In your opinion, are your perceptions of our company's core offerings accurate? Have they been validated? If so, how?

THE CLIENT OR PROSPECT'S PREFERRED EDUCATIONAL PROCESS—AND STRICT PROCUREMENT PROCEDURES

*I*F YOU WANT TO DO BUSINESS WITH OUR ORGANIZATION, HERE ARE OUR *rules and procedures for what your company needs to do to submit your product, service, or solution for consideration. In fact, these steps are posted right on our Web site, which I encourage you to visit at www.follow-our-rules-they-are-here-for-a-reason.com."*

If you have approached a larger company and been hit with this warm response to your courting efforts, get used to it. This is the way increasing numbers of large and midsized multinationals go about acquiring goods and services today. The fourth constraint, while it's always been an issue, is fast becoming a significant impediment to the margins of thousands of businesses throughout the world.

Employees of midsized and large corporations feel immense pressure to follow their companies' rules and guidelines for acquiring products and services. One or two missteps can lead to a reprimand by a manager or even job loss. This is nothing to mess with. Understandably, individuals you are attempting to call on take these rules and procedures very seriously. And they do not appreciate "some small business entrepreneur," salesperson, or anyone else who attempts to circumvent their procurement procedures. The interesting thing is that those of us who make our living in the selling profession often attempt to get by or around these rules and procedures because of the pressure on us to produce a number. So we're all in this together.

This constant constraint will not go away in our business lifetime. Indeed, it will become a bigger impediment over time, given how companies are streamlining their procurement procedures.

As the products, services, and solutions of certain industry verticals become perceived as commodity purchases, acquirers will build ever more elaborate procedures, rules, and mazes that potential suitors must follow and abide by as they attempt to gain business. This applies across industries as diverse as hotel/hospitality, information technology, accounting and audit services, office equipment, cell phones/PDAs/handheld wireless devices, insurance and financial services, health care, home entertainment electronics, and many other products and services.

Consider a one-hundred-million-dollar multiyear contract that a well-known multinational did not win. This involved copiers, document management solutions, and support services for one of the larger financial concerns in the country. One of the primary reasons they didn't win this account (according to the provider) had nothing to do with the value of their offerings. As one of the premier providers, they didn't get the business, as best they could tell after investing twelve to eighteen months in courting expenses, time, and attention, had to do with one guy in the procurement department who essentially scared the pants off them, saying that if they went "around him" and spoke to anyone in management, he'd make sure they didn't get the business.

Think this is baloney? Well, think again. Some procurement and purchasing departments of large corporations are wreaking havoc on providers trying to court their business. This dynamic causes deals to drag on, increases selling and marketing expenses, and reduces profit margins on the deals that do finally close after procurement is done hammering for the absolute best price, service, and support.

You as the vendor-provider often have to play by the rules set by procurement. Otherwise, you risk being excommunicated by the purchasing and procurement teams, who seem to take great delight in being the Rules Police—a power trip for some individuals in large organizations. Imagine what it's like trying to get into Wal-Mart, Target, or Best Buy. These companies know how you view them. They know you're thinking "If we can just get in there with one or two items, we can get a foothold, and then we're set."

The greater the procurement department's perception that your offerings are commodities, the tougher, more elaborate, more time intensive and expensive the courting and closing process can be for you and your company—and did I mention much less fun?

I have been through my fair share of these fire drills with large entities. Without question, it can be a major grind on the vendor-provider's time, efforts, resources, and spirit. And the larger the fish you are trying to catch, the more militaristic the rules and procurement procedures can become. Suffice it to say this fourth constraint is real and grows more complex every year, directly impacting your bottom-line profitability. There is hope, however. The Accelerants are tools that can help you attack this constraint in a multipronged manner, giving you more leverage over the situation, enabling you to navigate more efficiently in tough waters. Stand by.

THE CLIENT OR PROSPECT'S EXECUTIVE-LEVEL DECISION-MAKING PROCESS

*T*HIS FIFTH CONSTRAINT TO YOUR BUSINESS'S GROWTH IS COUPLED tightly with the fourth. Together, they can create a large crevasse that envelops providers already working effectively with their contacts inside an organization. They've been fighting the good fight, trying to respectfully move the task force of midlevel management's recommenders forward to the executive level. But senior executives and owners often have their own pattern and process for coming to a decision, signing off, and moving forward. Sometimes the two decision-making processes (lower to midmanagement versus executive level management) are aligned. Sometimes they are not. It is very difficult to know for certain.

What I mean is, the procurement process is usually quite defined after the task force or committee has issued the RFI or RFP (request for information/proposal), met with and vetted the potential vendors, and selected two finalists for procurement to go "beat up" and work out the details. Once these two "finalists" are presented up the chain of command to executive management for the final decision, this is when the vendor-providers learn that in some cases, the senior management may or may not have a formal decision process in place. And herein can lie the problem for those courting the business.

This dance of two or more distinct levels of management, with two or more procedures (defined or undefined) for making decisions, could be viewed as a grinder solely designed to squeeze and exhaust the poor vendor-providers as they attempt to find their way to the finish line. And some never make it. They fall into the crevasse because the companies they are hunting happen to be so sharp, and so methodical, they use these two decision-making procedures to do exactly that: grind out the absolute best deal.

This fifth constraint confuses business developers who have had their heads down, working diligently for months with mid-management people and below. They have spent time earning the prospect's trust, establishing rapport, presenting their wares, explaining how they can solve or address a stated business need, and benchmarking their offerings with live beta-test pilots, allowing the client to "test" their solution in a live environment when appropriate. They have also worked with the team (tasked by senior management to find, analyze, benchmark, and recommend two finalists) to build the business case that justifies the expenditure and expected return on investment (ROI). And then—everything comes to a halt.

It's like bringing a horse to the edge of the water and never letting it drink. This entire process drives managers and vice presidents of your company absolutely crazy as well, because for months, they've seen the call-detail reports documenting the results and action steps agreed to at each and every meeting.

As the midlevel management of the company you're courting finally decides, "It's time to bring this thing forward to senior management," the clock begins to tick. The management within your organization now gets the cue that the process seems to be moving forward, and it's as if somebody pulls out an egg timer and everyone stands around it, acutely aware if things begin to drag. And drag they can—big time—at this point. That's because the two decision processes are not aligned in many cases—either by accident or by design, you will never know. What you will know is that the decision processes will slow your growth. You will feel it.

As an example of how different and dysfunctional the mid-management and executive-level management decision-making processes can be, and how costly this can be to your company, consider what commonly happens when a large firm issues an RFP. A formal request for proposal for a particular product, service, or solution would seem to indicate they are interested in purchasing sometime in the not-too-distant future. Notice that I said "seem." It is not always the case that the company buys anything after putting the vendors through months of dancing on the head of a pin. The response from primary providers is to take the RFP seriously. In fact, often there's a buzz as the top-tier players begin to swarm the company that's issued an RFP of significant size.

As the recipient of my share of RFPs from large corporations, they are usually very detailed. The rules of engagement are usually spelled out, dictating what providers can and cannot do, who they can speak with, the date the proposal is due, who it should be sent to, and when (approximately) a decision will be made. But time and again, they don't answer all the questions vendors have, which causes the vendors to contact the task-force lead to gain additional clarification.

Even though this is all well and good, this form of "shopping" the marketplace creates a good deal of paranoia among providers. They generally know or figure out the other providers who received the same RFP. Often, this touches off subtle little attempts I'll call "friendship calls" from the senior management of each vendor who received the RFP. These calls are typically placed from VP levels within the vendor to VP levels or higher within the company that issued the RFP. And guess what? Sometimes, you get stonewalled, because they won't talk. They'll say something to the effect of, *"Hey, I appreciate your call, but to be very candid with you, the task force is in charge of this whole thing. They are running the RFP. So my advice is to contact them."*

This dead end drives providers crazy, because they actually do have a few questions, but they were also looking for *the scoop*—the inside angle on what the company is *really* looking for. For whatever reason, based on the behavior of courting vendors, it seems nobody trusts or wants to work with the task force, even though they know they have to. This is why providers will attempt to get some executive-level buy-in, or sponsorship, even though they know they are treading on dangerous ground.

So they get their hands slapped once in a while, and eventually figure out they should knock it off or risk being disqualified from the bidding process. So here we go: months and months of work responding, going to meetings, asking for more clarification, responding again, etc., etc. And when the decision comes out and it's against you, it's not uncommon for your company to attempt to blast in the door at an executive level to salvage the deal. Often in this scenario, the senior executives will not engage (even when it's your CEO who puts in the call), but instead, will often hide behind their task force.

I have experienced this myself because I used to do exactly that when we learned we weren't going to be awarded the business. I found it amazingly frustrating that there seemed to be such a well-coordinated effort between the lower part of the organization and senior management that it truly wore us out. Maybe that was the plan. It worked.

Be cognizant of this crevasse. It is subtle but deep, and when you fall in, it's difficult to recover. That is why this constraint can impede your ability to close. This was another area of pain that caused me to develop the Accelerants, which are designed to jump over, or at the very least, minimize this constraint, by reorienting the very manner in which you initially engage with clients and prospects. When you learn how to do that, this gap will be less of a constraint on your company's business development efforts.

YOUR MARKETING ORGANIZATION'S ARTICULATION OF THE MESSAGE AND VALUE PROPOSITIONS FOR YOUR CORE OFFERINGS—AND THE INCONSISTENCY WITH WHICH THEY ARE COMMUNICATED TO CLIENTS AND PROSPECTS

*THIS ONE IS A HUGE CONSTRAINT THAT PUTS A GREAT DEAL OF DOWN-*ward pressure on the ability to close business—and it is prevalent in organizations of *all* sizes.

If you do some soul-searching within your enterprise, you may find that factors squarely within your control—which you are either unaware of or are not acting on—are impeding your company's growth. Are your current value propositions full of nebulous but beautifully crafted words that articulate the benefits of your offerings without getting "granular" as to the financial impact or outcomes they could deliver for clients? And are you aware that your salespeople are using messages that may not have anything in common with those crafted by marketing? These problems *are* within your control, and yet are rarely dealt with in a cohesive manner inside companies. This is why this constraint can wreak havoc on getting more revenue in the door!

For whatever reasons, in both large and small firms, marketing and sales camps rarely work together. The marketing people are tasked to describe and articulate the message, net benefits, and value propositions of the offerings. They then hand these over to sales and business development, which will sometimes review them and say things like *"Clearly—they just don't get it, do they? What am I supposed to do with this? I don't think I'm even going to use this stuff."*

After working with Fortune 1000 organizations for more than ten years, I can tell you that generally speaking, the larger the corporation, the bigger the gap of disconnectedness between the sales and marketing organization, and the bigger this constraint. There's an unspoken air that some marketing organizations take on, appearing shielded and out of touch with the battle being fought on the street by their sales organization. This vibe radiates from some big marketing departments toward their salespeople and often feels to them like a lack of respect. If you're aware of this "attitude" within your own firm, you might be able to minimize this constraint's damage on your top-line revenues.

The topic of compensation also adds fuel to this constraint, making it even tougher to rein in. You see, in most cases, the marketing folks receive a straight salary, which helps insulate them, making them immune to the normal hiccups, hills and valleys of a typical sales cycle. Their incomes are constant—no interruptions, no spikes, no droughts. This can help foster a feeling and mentality within the marketing department that their jobs are safe and secure—a "glass house" attitude. I also think that, in some cases, the salaried marketing people resent the high salaries successful salespeople are able to command. They may also envy the travel, expense accounts, and the fact that producers are not so tied to their desks.

As you've probably guessed by now, the salespeople have their own perceptions of the value the marketing department plays in the company's life. Often, they feel the marketing department is highly overrated. These negative attitudes between the sales and marketing camps cause exactly that—separate camps. Silos form and feed into this self-perpetuating view of each other's worth (or lack thereof) to the organization. This spiraling constraint goes undetected within many companies until the numbers are consecutively missed by a large margin. But then it's too late. The CEO, SVP of marketing, and SVP of sales have already been shown the door.

If there are two organizations that had better get along with each other, it is these. They must develop a deeper appreciation for how each department makes the other's job better and easier, in the spirit of moving the company forward. The alternative is not a pretty picture.

If you are part of a smaller entity that doesn't have a marketing or sales department per se, and you are the one charged with developing the messages, this constraint still applies, because someone within your company will eventually approve or sign off on how you've articulated your company's offerings.

The question now becomes, Whose fault is it that the two camps rarely work together? I don't know, but laying blame never benefits anyone. However, because the sales and business development executives are on the street going toe to toe with clients and prospects, they—when asked—can shed valuable light on the value propositions and help shape what they are hearing on the street into messages that might be more salient and credible with the purchasing audiences.

Yes, it is challenging—especially in midsized and larger companies—to pull together some client executives and managers from the field with the marketing people, but the benefits are worth the effort. If your aim is to minimize the sixth constraint within your operation, then try this idea on for size.

Bring in some of the key people from your marketing and sales organization (the second Accelerant on page 100, provides a list of the people we suggest to involve), task them with working together, and watch how your value propositions take on new life and impact.

Remember, clients also enjoy helping out in this area because it makes them feel important and special. They can provide valuable feedback, giving you clues as to what makes them more interested in and attracted to your messages. Consider involving a few of them. And if you are a smaller entrepreneurial firm that can bring your people together with less effort, there is no excuse for neglecting this important exercise.

Let me share an example of the synergy and healing that can happen when a company brings together the senior marketing people with the senior sales, client account and regional managers, and a few top producers from the street. Several years back, a large multinational retained us to assess the value propositions (which had already been created by the marketing department) specific to an offering about to be launched in the United States. They wanted to determine if the propositions could be improved or tightened to be as effective as possible for the salespeople in the field.

The vice president of sales for the division hosted the meeting. In came the VP of marketing and a few people from his department, ready to discuss (and defend) the value propositions they had already nailed, in their opinion. The salespeople had not yet seen them. The workshop began with the understanding that we were all there to assess what had already been done and to determine if they'd "play" in the field.

If you've ever facilitated a group of high-level, advanced thinkers who are quite vocal with their opinions relevant to what will—and will not—work, then you understand that within about an hour, the spirit of "let's play nice" quickly disintegrated. I found myself playing traffic manager, designating who could speak and when. Everyone from the sales side of the house had an opinion about what had already been crafted. Some comments had merit, and some were downright harsh.

If you've ever been in a situation where you've done your level best on a project, then submitted it to others for review, then you understand how the marketing executive and his folks felt—attacked, underappreciated, and defensive. They began to think (I could just see it coming) that the salespeople simply did not get it. Period. The sales staff thought the same way about the marketing people. Neither team was listening to the other.

Then the salespeople began to explain and teach the marketing people why the current value propositions wouldn't pull with the audiences they were desperately trying to engage—and why, if the suggested tweaks and adjustments were made, the value propositions could work even better. We helped them articulate why the current version would fall on deaf ears, create zero urgency with buyers, and hurt everyone in the organization due to lack of sales.

When the marketing department saw the connection to their paychecks, they became less defensive, and the door opened to constructive teamwork around what needed to be tweaked and why. What came out of this client's session was a deeper understanding about what the sales organization is up against, and why they needed help from marketing in putting more teeth into the various value propositions and messages. I will talk more about this process in Accelerant principle number four, METRIC THE MESSAGE.

At the end of the meeting each person felt they had contributed to improving the current state of the company's messages, understood why the revamping was necessary, and why the messages would probably work much better in the field. A general sense of pride and accomplishment was easy to see on everyone's face.

And guess what—when these revised messages were launched, they worked. The bottom line is many organizations' messages and value propositions don't say anything, according to clients and prospects. The messages have no teeth—no numbers, ranges, or percentages—high side, low side—to back up their claims. Because of this serious void in most organizations' messages, and because there is typically little consistency with which they are communicated to clients and prospects between marketing collateral, brochures, white papers, Web site information, and what the sales organization is out there communicating, this constraint is hazardous to your revenue line. If undetected and left alone, it can infect your company, slowing down everything, and you won't know what the heck is going on.

SEVENTH CONSTRAINT
YOUR LEVEL OF ENTRY AND ENGAGEMENT WITHIN CLIENT AND PROSPECT ORGANIZATIONS

WHO DECIDES THE APPROPRIATE OR CORRECT LEVELS OF INDIVIDU-als to call on when approaching a prospect? Is it the prospect? Or do you, the person attempting to sell something, set the ground rules (especially since you may be footing the sales expenses of the business developers)? And how do the rules change when you are calling on an existing client? Who determines the proper levels of people to contact in this scenario?

After training senior executives and the sales and business developers of Fortune 1000 organizations for ten-plus years, what I see most frequently is that most companies leave it up to the salespeople to determine who to call on. Their attitude is *"This is what we pay you people to do, so figure it out—and if you miss your numbers, we'll deal with it at that point."* The senior management hasn't really gotten involved with analyzing the levels of people their sales, business development, and marketing people are calling on. They've been relatively hands-off in this area, not wanting to micromanage their salespeople. Let me explain why you might want to become a little more hands-on in this specific area if you wish to collapse your closing cycles and minimize or eliminate this constraint in your company.

The seventh constraint is a hotly debated area involving several parties' strongly held beliefs and opinions about how organizations should work—which is not the same as how they actually do work. There is never just one answer to the question of the most appropriate person to call on initially—or who the decision makers are. The real answer is that it depends. Who you target depends on the products, services, and solutions you represent to the marketplace, along with what you believe is the appropriate way to approach a prospect or client. People have deep-seated beliefs in this area, which directly impact little things like the length of your sales and closing cycle, the cost of the selling effort, and the margin you can command. I will say it again, because it is so important: The level of people you are targeting has a direct correlation to the length of your closing cycles and the speed at which you can bring in business. It directly impacts your time to a deal.

For the past decade, senior executives in Fortune 1000 client organizations have complained bitterly to me about the levels of their client and prospect relationships. Basically, they rant that they are not high enough inside prospect opportunities—even with current clients.

During the go-go nineties, getting an appointment with the right person wasn't really an issue because things were going well and money was flowing. Today, things are so different. Successful people realize this and are changing their approach strategies accordingly. But the unhappy lament I continue to hear from most senior executives is *"Why is it taking so long for our people to close an opportunity nowadays? Can someone please tell me? It's not like they haven't heard of us before. And why are our closing cycles stretching?"*

I have an answer and an opinion. It is because the business

developers and entrepreneurs are entering too low in the organization from the outset. Even when they have the *choice* to go in at any level, they typically enter the organization too low.

For example, many technology clients have the mind-set that because they are selling various technology solutions, the most appropriate place to enter a potential client is inside the technology department somewhere and to then find a sponsor or champion interested enough in the solution to lead the process of seeing if there is sufficient interest to make something happen. And even if they attempt to enter at the top of the IT organization, through the chief information officer/technology officer (CIO/CTO), this is not often where they land. Instead, they end up in some midlevel area within IT, which is where they begin their sales effort. Hence, there are typically a series of meetings (at a relatively low level inside the IT organization) before they know if there is any real possibility of doing any business.

However, clients have another choice, which is to craft and tailor their value propositions in a way that communicates the financial outcomes their solutions drive for clients, and then enter in the finance organization instead of the IT organization. We have done work like this with some of our technology clients, shaping the teeth inside their value propositions to be attractive and compelling to the financial officers inside their targeted firms, hence getting them in higher and faster in many cases, so they can have the type of conversations they want to have with prospective clients.

Much of the reasoning for these decisions to enter at a low level is tangled around three issues: individuals' belief about where they should start, their personal confidence level, and their belief in their company's offerings.

Believe it or not, salespeople and account managers sometimes wonder whether their products and services actually do produce positive net benefits for the customer. Can you see how this constraint is linked with others, especially the third constraint? Your team's perceptions and general confidence in their own solutions (the third constraint) directly impact where, and at what levels within a prospective client, they will target to enter. This impacts the speed at which you can close additional business, and at what margin. These two constraints are attached at the hip.

This seventh constraint is in a league all by itself. It is also very hard to detect. Why would your salespeople ever admit that they might need some help connecting with key decision makers a little higher in the companies they are targeting, when the assumption is they're supposed to know how to do that. That's what they're paid to do, right? The fact is, many salespeople are having trouble raising their level of conversations with senior-level people. Let me illustrate how this constraint rears its ugly head—and how it causes serious grief when forecasting quarterly revenues for your company, your shareholders, and Wall Street if you're a public company. By the time you experience the resulting pain and negative impact, it's usually too late to do anything, other than learn how to use the fifth Accelerant, ACCESS THE CASTLE, so you're not continually caught off guard when it comes to forecasting your revenues.

If you are an executive or business owner, think back over the last six months to the times you've done your "pipeline" or account reviews with each of your salespeople. This is the painstaking process of methodically reviewing opportunities and having your people explain the status of each deal as best they can. In particular, you make sure you hear the details of those opportunities that are 80 to 90 percent in the can, according to your salespeople—the deals that are as good as gold, with a time line to close within the next sixty to ninety days.

After finishing the pipeline/account review, you pay close attention to the progress updates of the deals you were told were "80 to

90 percent in the can" because you're counting on them to close. In fact, you may have already told the bank or your investors they were coming in. Thirty days later, you receive an urgent e-mail from your salesperson on the West Coast, saying he doesn't know what happened, but he lost "that large deal" that was basically "in the can." You fire an e-mail back saying you'll do whatever it takes to assist in salvaging the deal after you get briefed on the specifics.

You task your salesperson to e-mail you immediately with the contact information on the highest-level contact they've been working with during the last six to nine months so you can make contact—from a senior management level. In comes the e-mail. The highest-level contact is the director of customer relationship management (CRM) inside this multinational corporation. Your heart sinks because you know your ability to affect any change at this point with this level of person is next to zilch.

Kiss the deal good-bye. The odds are against your mixing it up with this contact to salvage the opportunity. How could you possibly impact the deal when your company is still so low in the organization? And furthermore, if you go blasting in to the top now, this late in the game, guess who looks like a poor loser?

With 20/20 hindsight, you finally understand why you were a bit edgy after going through each of your salespeople's pipeline reviews. Your instincts were telling you there might be a problem, but you couldn't put your finger on it. Now you know what the problem is. Your level of entry into client and prospect organizations is too low. You can imagine the grim downward spiral if this continues to happen. It will negatively affect your forecasting accuracy, your cash flow, and the level of your credit lines with the bank to cover the deals you thought were nailed, but aren't coming in.

There is plenty here to sort through and figure out. The Constraints Assessment helps you see how you and your people feel about this area of selling. At the end of constraints one through three I have provided a sampling of the questions that we use with clients. The entire assessment addresses all twelve constraints. Producers, their managers, and senior management often disagree about the appropriate person to engage with first because there is no one correct answer. So it's best to get the differences of opinion out onto the table in order to analyze everyone's views, which will help lead you to some answers that will minimize this constraint in your company. Our clients use the assessment tool to measure the level of pain around each of the constraints, which helps them uncover potential solutions that will work within their culture and collapse their closing cycles. For more information, you can visit www.accelerantinternational.com and click on the Constraints Assessment.

THE INABILITY TO ARTICULATE YOUR VALUE PROPOSITIONS TO THE REAL DECISION MAKERS

*I*F YOU BELIEVE THAT MOST FIELD SALES FORCES (EVEN A PARTY OF one) spend the better part of their day calling on and working with *decision makers,* I suggest you take two aspirin and lie down on the nearest couch before you read this next section, because it's probably not the case. Some buyers represent themselves as "the decision makers," when they are nothing more than a recommender with no direct control over purchasing your offerings. This constraint is tightly linked to the seventh (Your Level of Entry and Engagement). However, in those situations when you do "get in" at a high level, clients often *blow it* by falling back onto "safe" territory, meaning they revert to going through their PowerPoint presentation, which does nothing to answer the key questions the real decision makers have. Messages that help decision makers cut to "the financial net-net" that your offerings could provide. Therefore, even if salespeople are in front of the correct audience, they fail to articulate the real guts, the real outcomes their core offerings could deliver. Hence, real decision makers become frustrated and the downward spiral continues.

One of the mega rages of the eighties, championed by the most popular of management consulting and change management firms, was Total Quality Management (TQM). Integral to the TQM program was the concept of pushing the authority and decision-making capabilities down into the fingers of the organization to foster a more empowered, efficient, and cohesive entity. Driving the more basic decisions (and budget authority for those decisions) down into the organization would lessen the bottleneck at the top while increasing employees' feelings of belonging, ownership, pride, and commitment to the enterprise—this was the thinking at least, and it worked for a while.

However, this is *not* how many organizations operate today! A succession of global events has completely revamped the way people and companies do business. These include the dot-com bubble and bust, several natural disasters, the massive runup in the stock market and subsequent crash, the terrorist attacks on September 11, 2001, and the implosion of thousands of businesses between 2000 and 2004. Sweeping cutbacks and cost controls rapidly became the order of the day. The scale of corporate fraud and corresponding litigation resulting from some of these events has also added to the mix. As a result, this love affair with empowering the people seems to have all but disappeared.

Within thousands of companies large and small a power shift has occurred, stripping decision-making authority and the ability to spend money from lower and midrange managers, and consolidated it with a relative few at the top. Most producers, however, are not *playing* at the top of the companies they are working with. They are somewhere in the middle at best.

How can you expect to reduce your closing cycles and close business faster if you and your people are working primarily with recommenders? Few people will tell you they don't have the power to make a decision, which is part of the problem. You invest time working with those who say they have the ability to make the call—only to find out later (after spending several thousand in courting expenses) that they only have the ability to recommend.

Many organizations have expressed their frustration with this very real issue at their own management planning retreats, sales conferences, and the like. It has become so extreme in some organizations, it seems difficult to get a box of Kleenex signed off. Maybe a vice president could do it, unless it's over a few thousand dollars, and in that case it needs to go higher for approval and signoff. I'm being a tad sarcastic, but you get the point.

Because of this constraints impact on your ability to attract more revenue, I will state it again. The inability to articulate your value propositions to the real decision makers. Now stay with me as I draw a parallel. Often the salespeople don't like the message/ value propositions produced by the marketing department (the sixth constraint) because they're not compelling enough. The sales force may not even believe in their company's claims. Couple this with the fact that they are too low in the organizations they are courting—banging around with people who no longer have the power to make decisions, because the authority has been driven back up to the top—and you have a royal and expensive mess. This is a big issue for companies, directly impacting their costs related to gathering business. How does your company fare in this area?

Here are some observations of this constraint's ability to suppress your top-line growth. They come from several years of working with sales and marketing, business development, client account teams, and strategic growth executives inside Fortune 1000 and midsized organizations:

Fear of Rejection: The sales, business development, and marketing engines of many organizations have been lulled to sleep. They've become afraid of being perceived as too aggressive, too excited, and too confident about how their products or services can drive more value for the client.

This is sad, but isn't it the primary job of the business developer to bring more business your way? If you're going to learn how to get in front of more qualified decision makers faster and more frequently than you are now (Accelerant principle five, Access the Castle), why wouldn't you take full advantage of the opportunity by coming across as confident, decisive, and articulate about how much your offerings will benefit the client? These buyers *want* you to tell them—they are begging for it, because it is so hard for them to determine how one option is better than another.

Instead, many salespeople cop an expression that looks as if they just ate a bad meal, don't feel well, and are about to explode. You know the look: puppy-eyed concern. To illustrate this subtle trance that's come over some sales organizations in the last ten years, here's a quick story.

I was training a national sales organization (several hundred producers) of a multinational provider of payroll processing services and other related offerings. As we discussed ideas about how to add more power and TEETH to their existing value propositions they responded, "We can't say that."

"Why?" I asked. "You've been delivering leading-edge results to clients for more than twenty years now." To which they said, "Well, yeah, we have. I mean, I think we have. I'm sure we have, but to be sure, we really should ask our clients, because we don't track the results that closely. And many times, the clients won't tell us what they're actually getting."

Can you feel the lack of energy and accompanying lack of sales? My advice to those who want to be more articulate when in front of people who can actually say yes is, "You better start tracking the results your products and services deliver if you expect to be articulate with decision makers. No one else will do it for you, that's for certain."

Fear of Being Wrong: Here's a question for you: If senior executives and Wall Street analysts are wrong once in a while, and still operate just fine, why do salespeople have to be right all the time?

Who is putting all this pressure on the producers? Maybe it's your legal counsel who's scaring the sales force by making sure nobody is making claims that cannot be substantiated. But let's not forget that buyers are begging for this. So to avoid any trap, and keep your lawyers happy, pay attention to what I will teach in Accelerant principle four, METRIC THE MESSAGE. It will give you some concrete ideas and solutions to this constraint so that you no longer have to fear being wrong or being rejected and you will be able to present your value propositions to people who can actually say yes more frequently.

Remember, potential buyers are dying for someone—anyone—to be strong and aggressive with them. They want someone so excited about their company's offerings, their passion comes across on their face. Someone who has the guts to stand up and say, "*Yes. We can help you do this or that, and here's how or why.*" The Accelerants will give you the tools to help you do exactly that.

YOUR FEAR OF SUFFICIENTLY PREQUALIFYING THE CLIENT OR PROSPECT TO JUSTIFY ADDITIONAL MEETINGS DOWNSTREAM

*U*NLESS YOU'VE BEEN INVOLVED IN A HOT INDUSTRY, MANY PEOPLE feel that business has become tougher over the last several years: more of a slow grind, as some would describe it. Closing basic transactions such as presenting straightforward, low-end products or services that are not very expensive seems to take longer, cost more, and has become more complex than necessary. The pressure seems to be up on everyone. Wall Street appears intent to pound on publicly held companies, pushing for more top-line growth because CEOs have primarily focused on slashing costs, departments, and people during the early 2000s.

Organizational processes and procedures, leaders, and outside influencers have also been under the microscope in the quest to identify inefficiencies that can be resolved. And, generally speaking, an increased level of fear has crept into many people's decision-making processes, whether they will acknowledge it or not. Many of us are not consciously aware of how our decisions, or lack of them, have become interwoven with a dose of uncertainty and doubt.

Fear can help drive change, for better or worse. But in a tough business climate where fear is up it is no surprise that people trying to grow their businesses and close more deals have become more gun-shy. Perhaps a better word is *paranoid*. Paranoid of pushing too hard for the deal and irritating prospects in the process. Paranoid of being too aggressive with clients for more business in the quest for that ideal, strategic relationship.

Clearly, over the last few years, clients have gained even more leverage, power of choice, and purchasing assistance (if they have a procurement department) than smaller companies that do not have the manpower or procedures in place to "shop" the vendor options available in a methodical manner. But because of global competition, buyers have several good options available to them, and in many cases, they often come to believe that any selection among the top three to five providers would serve them well. This enables them to study their options, take their time, and run the search-and-selection process in a manner they deem appropriate. Contrast this current reality to the 1980s and go-go 1990s when, if you were selling any type of product, service, or solution, it was simply smart business to make sure the client or prospect was sufficiently prequalified, sometimes even before agreeing to a first meeting, a second, or certainly a third. It was important to draw out this information from the prospect before investing in additional downstream meetings to appease the boss.

Today, however, the dynamic is altogether different. It has become tougher across many industry sectors to bring in business. Put a prospect through your prequalification rigor nowadays, prior to having a second, third, or fourth meeting, and watch some go invisible. They will neglect to return your phone calls or give you one of several popular reasons why they've elected not to continue forward, at least with your firm.

They know very well that, in the majority of cases, *they* are in the driver's seat, and *they* call the next steps with vendor-providers. Based on the last few years of trends, if a prospect senses any resistance or pushback from the vendor, you can kiss meeting number two or three good-bye. This is the ninth constraint in the raw: not being able to properly prequalify your client or prospect at a time that makes good business sense to you, for fear that the client may halt the process altogether.

The buyer's increased level of power and leverage and the vendor's increased trepidation about prequalifying too aggressively and scaring away the prospect leave a gap. This gap can impede your growth because clients and prospects can exploit it. Closing cycles get longer, courting costs increase, and margins get thinner. In the years ahead, as this trend becomes more pronounced, this constraint will become an even bigger issue. Accelerant principles seven, eight, and nine will give you tools that will show you how to prequalify the prospect or client in the first couple of meetings by getting them to give you the relevant data or information you need. Then you can come back in meetings two or three and present a minibusiness case showing at a high level how your products, services, or solutions can help them—financially. This approach will also help you smoke out prospects that are wasting your time and energy.

YOUR FEAR OF LEADING THE DANCE WITH CLIENTS AND PROSPECTS

*T*HIS CONSTRAINT IS TIGHTLY COUPLED WITH THE NINTH (FEAR OF sufficiently prequalifying the client or prospect to justify additional meetings downstream) and linked with that good old emotion called fear.

It is impossible to lead the dance when you are not willing to communicate the financial outcomes that your core offerings could deliver the client, which then allows you to more thoroughly prequalify the opportunity by gaining the specific data you need from them to justify additional meetings downstream. This is what I mean by "Leading the Dance."

Most popular consultative sales training programs and process models teach that the professional, appropriate, and effective way to engage a potential buyer is to ask them questions about themselves, their business, areas of concern or pain, and their overall goals and objectives. As a result, the entire courting paradigm lets the client or prospect drive the process. They—not you—are leading the dance at every turn.

This is the way most of us have been trained and conditioned to sell. So how could this approach, which is so commonly used, actually be a constraint? Consider this typical scenario:

Derek Stone is a strappingly fit, six-foot-three, elegantly dressed, articulate, fifty-year-old, Ivy League–educated vice president of sales. He's one of six VPs of sales within North America. A custom-suit man, with crisp, white, custom-made French-cuffed shirts that could give you a paper cut if you got too close, he is the picture of "sharp." He has just put in a seven-year stint with a large technology provider. Derek has managed one hundred salespeople in his region, created his own sales process (borrowed from different training vendors during his seven-year stint), and put in a stunning performance this past year, collectively producing a 20 percent decline in annual topline sales—going from $250 million to this year's $200 million.

Just in time to avoid the fallout, Derek's been recruited away from this giant to become senior vice president of global sales for a thirty-million-dollar privately held technology firm with fourteen salespeople. The firm has an eye on a public offering if they can get to fifty million in sales relatively quickly.

The founder-owner and CEO of this profitable tech firm called Rock Solid Technologies is falling all over himself to put in place the total package to entice Derek away from his fancy position with the giant firm. With health-care coverage for his family, a respectable base salary, bonus, and stock options all nailed down, Derek accepts and moves his family from the East Coast to Minneapolis, where his role and opportunity to impact change is greater, he tells himself, his friends, and wife of twenty years.

Derek's bringing his big-company experience and trusty seven-point step-by-step sales process—the one that served his huge employer especially well during the past year by missing his number by fifty million dollars. He was able to minimize this unfortunate event with the new CEO, who was so enamored they were getting a big-company man, nothing else mattered.

So welcome Derek into his new role as SVP of global sales for Rock Solid Technologies. Upon getting his team of fourteen producers together at their first sales meeting, he introduces his trusty sales process. Bright-eyed and impressed, everyone eagerly jumps on board, committing to use and follow the process, which appears to be common sense:

Step One: Engage the prospect or client to understand their core business challenges and pains and to determine if they'd like to do anything about them relative to achieving their goals and objectives faster, better, or cheaper.

Step Two: Define the advocate, champion, coach, or executive sponsor inside the prospect or client company to assist them in scoping and better defining the potential opportunities.

Step Three: Build the team that will meet with the prospect or client team to further scope and define the opportunity in preparation for proposal creation.

Step Four: Proposal creation and pricing.

Step Five: Presentation of proposal to prospect/client.

Step Six: Negotiation of proposal, and acceptance.

Step Seven: Submit contract for review, acceptance, approval, and funding.

Since it has been battle-tested by a major corporation, the fourteen salespeople and CEO sign off on the process, and everyone goes about their business of targeting their whale-size opportunities.

Fast forward nine months into Derek's new role, and find the owner of Rock Solid utterly frustrated. For some reason, which Derek cannot explain to the CEO's satisfaction, 60 percent of the deals in the pipeline are taking twice as long to close. The prospect and client advocates are not even at vice-president levels, and the salespeople are getting mired in Step Three (Build the Team). In fact, the owner is livid about the massive spike in selling expenses, finding his people flying all over God's creation, taking multiple people to each meeting. To top things off, the CEO learns there's a pattern emerging where the salespeople are having two, three, sometimes four "meeting number threes" with many of the opportunities—some never advancing into Step Four of the seven-step sales process.

Instead of seeing the company grow and prosper, they're going backward at a pretty good clip. "*How could this be happening?*" the CEO says to himself. "*I brought in a top-notch guy to take this company to the next level. Instead, we are worse off than we were before Derek got here. What in the heck is going on here?*" Perhaps you know the answer if you've witnessed something similar in your career. Truth be told, it's happening in all industry sectors, with companies both public and private.

Before we dissect this seven-step sales process, can you guess where the holes are and how this relates to the question of who is leading the dance? Let's see what we come up with, since hindsight is 20/20.

Does Step One define the level or title of the person/people they must engage with in their first meetings with a client or prospect? And if they can't engage at that level, does it provide "rules" as to what to do in this situation (e.g., stop all together, call for reinforcements)? No, it does not. Does Step One instruct the salespeople to go into meeting number one with an articulate, financially oriented value proposition that communicates the basics of how Rock

Solid could help the prospect or client, within a general range? No, it does not.

Instead, it allows the salespeople to go in at any level, searching for the pain or general business problem, and determine if the prospect or client has enough urgency to do anything about it. If your experience is anything like mine, you have probably been in situations where the prospect *does not even know* if they are in pain or not. And in these situations, guess who gets to pay the price—meeting, after meeting, after meeting, after meeting—to help them figure out if there's any pain or not? You and your company.

We haven't even gotten to Step Two. Do you see why, in this approach, there is no way the salespeople will ever be able to control or affect the cost of sales, the amount of time it takes to bring a deal in, the pace at which the prospect or client moves forward—or the number of meetings that will take place? The answer is because they are not in control of anything; consequently, they are not leading the dance!

Can you see why Derek's attitude is, "It will take as long as it takes"? That is what he's been used to. But the CEO of Rock Solid has other ideas. Some changes are forthcoming. Derek's honeymoon with small company U.S.A. is over.

Who does this seven-step process impact? Basically everyone in this thirty-million-dollar firm, wouldn't you say? Except Derek, of course. Sensing the CEO's frustration, he contacted the recruiter in month eight of his tenure and lined up another position with a huge firm, with people who appreciate him and what he brings to the party. Derek's view is that it's the CEO of Rock Solid who just doesn't understand what it takes to grow an organization—or that he is unwilling to do what it takes to get into the big leagues.

It's amazing how frequently this scenario is playing itself out in companies of all sizes in North America and abroad—all because vendors are afraid to lead the dance.

In a nutshell, it is very difficult to lead the dance (laying out a specific step-by-step course of action in terms of downstream meetings and action steps for each meeting) when you do not present the prospect or client in the very first meeting with some level of clarity around how you could benefit them financially. And when you don't, it is virtually impossible to control the length, duration, and urgency (or lack thereof) of their meetings and calls with you. The Accelerants will provide you with multiple solutions to this common constraint so that it does not happen as frequently to you and your firm.

It's difficult to take back some of this control in meetings because clients and prospects are used to leading, calling out next steps with vendor-providers—assuming the initial dance with your company was a good experience. But more control helps close business faster.

Are you beginning to see why it might be a good idea to learn how to lead if you want to control your sales and marketing costs and shorten closing cycles? You cannot lead the dance if the value propositions you lead with don't have compelling financial business benefits enticing the client's attention—meaning they have no TEETH. And how can you drive the process if you enter at a level where the people you're dealing with don't even care if the message has any TEETH (seventh constraint)?

One last time: It is difficult to lead a client or prospect down a specific path or course of action under a reasonable time horizon if there are no clear, compelling financial business benefits as the main theme or focus of your meetings. Where is the urgency you are creating? It isn't there. And if it is not present, how can you realistically expect to compress your company's closing cycles?

The Constraints Assessment can help reveal how your business developers view the initial dance with the client or prospect—very important because it will also help you understand if you've got the right people on board. In your people's responses may lie the keys that you can combine with certain Accelerants to compress your company's closing cycles and overall cost of sales.

THE CONTENT, FORMAT, AND DELIVERY OF YOUR POWERPOINT PRESENTATION IS LACKLUSTER— TOO LONG AND NOT TIGHTLY FOCUSED

FOR MANY COMPANIES THEIR BOILERPLATE POWERPOINT PRESENTAtion is a sacred cow. It's their story, mission statement, description of products and services, clients served, and successes carved. A beautiful and cohesive footprint of the company—right? You would think so, based on how defensive some become when you start suggesting changes to their presentation.

They react as if you are making mean comments about their children. This is a strange response because when asked how they actually like their own boilerplate, they typically reply: *"It's all right, but too long . . . It's boring . . . My prospects tune out in the middle . . . There's to much information in there that they don't seem to care about . . . It's not very exciting . . . It's our standard pitch, and we're not authorized to change anything in it."*

If the people giving the presentation are not proud or impressed with it, is it fair to expect that the recipients should be? To bring it even closer to home, ask your people to be candid with their opinions about your company's presentations. This conversation may help you understand why so many companies are finding (once they commit the time to look into it), that this particular element of their sales process actually interferes with closing more business.

In fact, many companies' standardized boilerplates are substantial blockades to future growth. Their deck contains too many slides, takes too long to get through, is not tailored to the level of executives it's being given to, and very often the *meat* is stuffed toward the end of the presentation, which irritates senior executives. The presentation also typically contains too much unnecessary detail. Look into your presentation to assess if there's extraneous data.

The results may be speaking for themselves in terms of client and prospect reactions and your closing percentages. However, the good news is each component of your presentation can be altered or changed, because you have the power to change the elements that don't serve your purpose.

The Constraints Assessment questions can provide a gut check on what your people think of your presentations—and where they think the material could be enhanced. This is valuable data that can provide a measurable ROI if you act upon these suggestions.

To work on eliminating this constraint in your company flip to DELIVER THE ULTIMATE PRESENTATION on page 133—Accelerant principle six. It is a field-proven format and methodology for improving upon the current version of your standardized boilerplate. It will show you a specific methodology, and ideas on how to re-order and shorten the content while adding pizzazz and power to your delivery. Fifteen years of consistent feedback from clients and prospects leave little doubt that this proven format is a winner. In fact, senior executives particularly love it.

TWELFTH CONSTRAINT

YOUR INABILITY TO COMMUNICATE TO CLIENTS AND PROSPECTS—THE FINANCIAL BENEFITS OF WORKING TOGETHER

WHICH IS SMARTER: HELPING PROSPECTS AND CLIENTS UNDER-stand early on in your courting process the possible financial deliverables, outcomes, or net-nets of your products, services, or offerings or allowing them to figure it out when they say they are ready to? Strangely, most people do it the second way.

If you drill down to its very essence, this constraint negatively impacts and effectively blocks many organizations' revenue growth plans for two primary reasons:

1. The people you are selling to are being pressured by their organizations to deliver results through every product, service, or solution they consider purchasing.

2. The inability of providers to articulate how their products or services create or deliver financial benefit, impact, or business value for the prospect and client.

The twelfth constraint is the result of a sales process that lets the prospect or client lead the dance for three reasons:

1. The provider lacks confidence in their offerings' ability to produce a financial benefit.

2. The provider doesn't feel they need or should commit to financial claims up front because they believe it's the prospect's or client's responsibility to figure it out. In some cases, the provider's legal counsel is telling them they cannot—in any form or fashion—put out numbers or commit to specifics. The key word here is *commit*. (I will address this in Accelerant principle four, METRIC THE MESSAGE, since there is a solution to the problem.)

3. The provider is having difficulty determining the financial benefits of their products and services and then believing in them enough to make a compelling presentation.

This is a real issue for many companies. The larger question is: Why should you take a close look at this in your organization? The answer is simple. If you do business in a very competitive industry where clients have multiple attractive alternatives to your products and services, they may view you pretty much the same as they view other top providers. If there is any chance of this happening, they will cop the attitude that the top vendor-providers' features and benefits look pretty darn close—almost vanilla, in their assessment. At that point in the process, the provider is likely to hear something like this:

"Look Michael, at the end of the day, clearly your stuff is very good. We like how our relationship has progressed; there's been a good history here, etc. But we have a few alternatives we have to look at as well. What we really need from you is to help us understand the financial business benefits of your products and services. That,

more than anything, will help us assess the direction in which we should go."

Now let's rewind to the beginning of this chapter. The people you are selling to are under immense pressure to show results for what they are buying, or considering buying. Because the features and benefits of each option are becoming more and more blurred among top vendor choices, clients and prospects are having trouble seeing any substantial differences. Therefore, the easiest, fastest, and *safest* way for them to justify a purchase is by understanding the financial business benefits of your offerings.

The faster and earlier in the process they can understand this, the better. If you aren't willing to do this work for them or help them figure it out in terms they understand and accept, this constraint is absolutely impacting your growth. This is important enough to discuss with your colleagues to get their perspective.

Accelerant principle four, METRIC THE MESSAGE, will provide tools to help you better articulate how your offerings can financially impact prospects and clients so that you can minimize this constraint.

You have now been exposed to the twelve constraints, and the way they slow down or block your firm from achieving more top-line growth in a reduced time horizon. Understanding these twelve road blocks and dealing with those that apply to you and your organization will assist you in hitting the targets you set for yourself and your company. They all directly impact your ability to bring in revenue, and the speed at which you are able to get it in the door— something Wall Street is always keenly interested in, as you already know.

You may already have an inkling as to which constraints are the biggest impediments in your company. These constraints continue to hold up forward progress in thousands of companies of all sizes.

The key is determining which ones might be negatively impacting your growth. The faster you figure out which ones are the biggest issues for your business, the quicker you can address them.

It is now time to take a look at the Accelerants—the principles that can address and minimize your constraints and take your business development efforts to the next level.

Section Two:
The Accelerant Principles

*TWELVE PROVEN PRINCIPLES TO OVERCOME,
MINIMIZE, OR DISSOLVE THE CONSTRAINTS
TO YOUR BUSINESS'S GROWTH*

*B*ECAUSE THERE'S SO MUCH NOISE IN OUR LIVES, WE ALL NEED TO BE reminded of why we are investing our precious time in this or that so we can stay the course and learn whatever it is we are attempting to learn.

We've now examined each of the twelve constraints, discussing how and why they wreak major havoc on the speed at which you are able to pull in more business and increase your cash flow. Before I share each of the Accelerant tools, I want to give you a another taste of how effective and necessary this process is if you want your messages to be heard faster, by the right levels of decision makers, to get a decision in less time. That's what *Accelerants* is really all about.

So before I take you through each individual tool—each Accelerant—explaining each one's value and the benefit each one can deliver by itself or in concert with others as a cohesive process, here is a story about the application of the process on an opportunity of significance that made real money.

Accelerants helped my partner and me close a seven-figure deal with Household Finance International—after they had already selected one of our competitors at the conclusion of an exhaustive RFP process (which we were not part of). Back when we courted them, they were approximately seven or eight billion in annual revenues. Now they are even bigger, called HFC-Beneficial, and part of an even larger concern, HSBC Finance. This story will show you the power behind these tools and how they can work very effectively at helping you bring home more bacon.

ACCELERANT SUCCESS STORY: IT'S NEVER TOO LATE

"Somehow we missed it. How did we miss an RFP submission from Household Finance?" I couldn't believe it. Why didn't we know about this opportunity? Why weren't we sent their RFP? Upon securing a copy of the request for proposal, we learned that HFC had already selected one of our toughest competitors, installed two systems in their collections center in the West, and were continuing the rollout to other centers within their U.S. operations. This opportunity was over, dead, sewn up. The task force had disbanded, and from what we could find out, the installation and integration rollout was on schedule, moving forward without a hitch—a totally missed opportunity.

We went through the RFP, trying to find a clue as to why this competitor was selected, and came across something strange. Many times within the document, HFC stated they wanted an IBM-based predictive-dialing platform because they were a large IBM shop. The only thing strange was the task force had selected a non-IBM-based platform vendor. We were the only IBM-based platform in this market at that time. Even though we were not privy to the details, something didn't seem right.

What could we do? From what we could glean through the

grapevine, they'd already made their decision and were well on their way, with an installation, integration and migration schedule running smoothly to boot.

Did we dare do an Accelerant Blitz on this organization? And if we did, who would we target, since the task force had disbanded and was probably back to business as usual? Plus, if we did get in with someone with enough power and authority who would listen and take action, what would our excuse be—our reason for stirring up the waters? Could it be that the task force made an error in their selection process? Why didn't they select an IBM-based platform if that was a key requirement? This became our crack in the door, our justification for approaching them with a "Did you know?"-type message to the highest levels of this organization—levels well above where the task force rested.

Risky? I didn't know. What would be wrong with a well-written COL System approach letter (you will learn about the Circle of Leverage System approach in Accelerant five) addressed to multiple senior executives who, we guessed, would want to know this? We would open with an introduction of our organization, followed by:

1. An apology for being unaware of their RFP

2. New information, telling them we had read the RFP, were aware they were searching for IBM-based predictive-dialing technology, and that according to our understanding, they had selected a non-IBM-based technology as their vendor of choice and had begun installation

3. A gridlike feature and benefit comparison of our systems against the vendor they'd selected—stressing that we were the only ones offering an IBM-based platform

4. Our offer—round-trip airfare, hotel, and meals for up to five people from their organization to join us in Atlanta, where they would see

two customer sites of our IBM-based installations in financial institutions

We spent time building metrics into the message, combined with the obvious benefit of offering an IBM-based platform.

ASSESSING OUR STATUS regarding this opportunity showed that we had no status. If we chose to approach, we needed a darn good, compelling value proposition articulating how they could still gain by coming over to our solution. DESIGNING OUR FUTURE forced us to analyze and focus on who we had to be in front of to cause action around our message. This also helped us identify who we needed to keep away from—those we felt would kill our chances faster than we could blink.

We analyzed the management structure and corporate research to solidify the points of entry inside this castle we would appeal to. We had CHARTERED OUR COURSE. Time to METRIC THE MESSAGE.

The RFP provided enough of an overview of the operation that we were able to craft a financial picture for our Circle of Leverage letter, which we hoped would garner the right executives' attention. The calibration of TEETH in the value proposition was time well spent. It's never a good idea to blast in the door at a high level—or any level—if you have nothing of compelling significance to offer.

The financial picture we painted was comparable to that of the vendor already selected. But because we provided the only verifiable IBM-based predictive-dialing platform at that time, there could be additional IT benefits, creating an even better financial business case for moving to our system solution.

ACCESSING THE CASTLE was going to be an artful strategy and dance, since this was a multibillion-dollar organization. We targeted the EVP of worldwide operations, who appeared through numerous direct reports to have ultimate responsibility for the business unit that would use our system. We also targeted senior financial executives and the SVP of credit and collections—staying clear of the technology organization upon initial entrance into the castle. Appealing to the IT organization (which appeared to hold half the placeholders on the task force) would only put us in quicksand. Typically, large IT organizations are stretched thin, with numerous projects that need to be done "yesterday" and little time to focus on prospective new vendors or suppliers.

The five-to-six-page COL System letters landed simultaneously on the desks of the targeted executives. Our request for initial access was a fifteen-minute conference call with the EVP of worldwide operations or one of the senior financial or collections executives— someone with the power, fortitude, and guts to reopen the task force analysis if it proved a prudent undertaking.

The letter was our best Hail Mary into this multinational. Even though our value proposition passed muster and was full of teeth, we had missed the party, which was our own fault. Persuading a group of disbanded task force members to come back together and review decisions they had already put to bed was definitely a Hail Mary approach.

With conviction solid and expectations in check, we waited two or three days as the COL letters percolated among the targeted executives like coffee in the morning. With the COL, you always follow up from the top down. When I followed up with the executive assistant to the EVP of worldwide operations, I learned he had seen the letter, discussed it with someone, and was willing to speak to us in about one week. Once the conference call was scheduled, we stopped all follow-ups with the others, since we had been granted access to one of the highest executives we had appealed to.

The phone call was brief and to the point. His overarching

question was *"Is this letter true? How can this letter be true? What do you mean that you are the only IBM-based predictive-dialing platform?"* As we said yes to his first question, I recall him barking out something to the effect that *"then how could our people have possibly missed that? I can't believe this. Gentlemen, I am going to take you up on your offer of flying five of our people to meet you in Atlanta to take a site tour of your IBM-based installations. Sit tight and my office will get back with you on the names and titles of those I want going on this little junket, and if they verify that what you are saying is correct, we will determine at that point what direction to take. Are we clear?"*

As we hung up, I thought we might actually have an opportunity. Within a couple of weeks, we had the names of five people and their respective titles. We quickly made flight arrangements and site visits with our two Atlanta-based clients.

On the day we greeted them at our manufacturing location in Atlanta, it was apparent they were not pleased to be there. Clearly, this was a case of being told by higher-ups to learn about a solution they had not considered for whatever reason. Now they had to investigate it and report back with their findings, though they had already made their decision months earlier.

The day was an exercise in rapport building. We apologized for not being aware of their RFP as they made cracks about what a hassle it would be to reopen the assessment. We remained humble and firm, stressing the IBM-based architecture behind our solution. We emphasized that because they were a large IBM shop, they could gain further economies of scale and performance.

The customer visit went smoothly but as we put them back on the plane, we had absolutely no feeling about whether we had budged them one inch. Now we waited for further direction.

It came from the EVP's office. We were to call the SVP of credit and collections for their Canadian operation. We were to fly up there and make a presentation explaining why they should work with us versus the selected vendor, since they were months from having their systems installed in Montreal, Toronto, and Vancouver.

We quickly found ourselves in Canada doing exactly as we were told. Several IT-oriented meetings followed with their Canadian operation, and lo and behold, we were awarded their Canadian collection centers.

We couldn't build the systems fast enough. As they were installed and integrated, performing as promised, guess where we were referred? To their credit and collections operation in the United Kingdom, also a large IBM shop. Suffice it to say, we were awarded that business as well, circling back to the U.S. operation to secure a toehold there. This proved a struggle, since they were well down the road with the original vendor. The important question is: Could we have gotten any of HFC's business had we not ASSESSED OUR STATUS, DESIGNED OUR FUTURE, METRICED THE MESSAGE so the offer was crystal clear, and then ACCESSED THE CASTLE by approaching their IT organization? No way would we have gotten five people to Atlanta had we approached their IT organization—not a chance. But based on how and where we did enter the castle, coupled with the tone and honesty of our approach letter, the message found its audience quickly with an executive who had the power to act.

DELIVERING THE ULTIMATE PRESENTATION, PAINTING THE FINANCIAL PICTURE, and HOLDING OUR GROUND (you'll become familiar with these ACCELERANTS shortly) were some of the additional reasons we were awarded portions of their business. In the end, we never got the U.S. business, but we did win their Canadian and United Kingdom business—a very satisfying result based on the size of the contracts.

Was it too late for us to approach in this situation? Is it ever too late to approach? Our results spoke for themselves. It wasn't too late, even though a few feathers were ruffled. Most important, HFC benefited in the final analysis—Accelerants to the rescue.

Which opportunities on your plate might warrant some form of Accelerant initiative? This is something to discuss with your peers. You may salvage opportunities you thought were already gone.

Now it's time to tell you about each Accelerant and how they can be used individually or together on opportunities of significance to grow your business.

ASSESS YOUR STATUS

*W*HEN YOU DON'T FEEL WELL AND THINK SOMETHING MIGHT BE wrong, you typically go to the doctor and tell them about your symptoms. They take the information and ask detailed questions, create a diagnosis, and advise you of treatment options. You weigh the options, ask clarifying questions if you want more insight, then select the treatment option that best suits your objectives. Your decision takes into account how much discomfort you are in, how fast you want it to go away, and the amount of money you are willing to spend to resolve the pain and the problem. This process is clean, fairly straightforward, full of common sense, and typically works well most of the time.

So why would you not follow the same pattern for your business when you think something is wrong? We're talking about your business—the vehicle that provides the income that funds your medical care and well-being. And just as you make decisions about your health, you should apply common sense here as well.

Now that you've had a taste of the constraints and how they can significantly impede your company's ability to create more revenue

ASSESS YOUR STATUS

in a more efficient manner, doesn't it make sense to do a basic assessment—a clean, straightforward process that will gather feedback from multiple parties (like you and your key people) and ask additional questions for clarification? A process that will then consolidate the data and present it back with an analysis of "what's going on" with the front end of your business relative to the constraints that are causing your business the most pain? This would allow you to make some decisions about which ones you'll tackle first.

Implementing strategies you believe will grow your business before assessing your status isn't the wisest thing you can do—wouldn't you agree? The assessment helps you understand what's below the water line—factors you might not see for the reasons I have shared in the description of each constraint. Then you'll become aware of the constraints impacting your growth, so you can address them with treatment options that fit your objectives, time lines, and budget.

Though there's never a convenient time for an assessment, procrastination isn't an option anymore. Top-line growth is the mantra—the new focus for companies large and small for the foreseeable future. CEOs and owners have trimmed the excess. There's nothing more to trim. Nobody's allowed to hide and the front end is the focus now. This means increasing business from existing clients and winning more business from prospects and vertical sectors you have yet to penetrate. This is what will take center stage from now on.

You may have heard the saying "The definition of insanity is doing the same thing over and over again but expecting a different result." If growing your business is a top priority, then Dr. Stephen R. Covey's principle, First Things First, from his book *The 7 Habits of Highly Effective People,* is relevant here. ASSESS YOUR STATUS. Learn which constraints are slowing down your growth, assess their severity, and select the treatment options that support your desired outcomes.

The questions following the first three constraints chapters are from the Constraints Assessment. Information on the complete version can be found at www.accelerantinternational.com. This will help you start the crucial conversation inside your company to find out what you and your people believe about each constraint's negative impact on your business. Therefore, you may want to go back and review the questions we use in the assessments for constraints one, two, and three.

For the sake of your business, you need to know how existing clients and prospects will answer these questions. So be direct and ask them. Their answers will go a long way to assist you in building strategies to enhance and lengthen your business relationships. And remember, their answers will be different, based on their relative power and authority within the organization. So it might be a good idea to group the executives and mid- and lower-level managers into similar "authority buckets" as you ask the questions.

The Constraints Assessment includes questions that address all twelve constraints. The sample questions for the first three constraints will help you begin the conversations within your company. My advice, if you want to do things right to minimize any surprises down the road, is to complete the assessment of all twelve constraints so you have a diagnosis of how each one is impacting your growth. Then you can address those causing the most pain and discomfort to the business before applying the appropriate Accelerants.

SECOND ACCELERANT PRINCIPLE
DESIGN YOUR FUTURE

NOW THAT YOU HAVE ASSESSED YOUR STATUS, KNOW WHICH CON-straints are impacting your growth, and determined how you will address them, it's time to decide how you want your new business-gathering process model to look and work going forward. The best way is to put the spotlight on the way you've been doing it the past several years—contrasting the current model with how you want your revised process to function.

One way to do this that works well is to come together by business unit. (If you're a smaller firm with a few products and services, gather the whole team together.) Owners; executives responsible for sales, marketing, and new business generation; key field sales managers; and a few key producers should come together to discuss internally focused questions such as:

1. How can we shorten our current selling cycle with clients and prospects we wish to target, collapsing our time to a deal?

2. Who (by title) are we calling on in our initial meetings and why?

3. Are these individuals the right people to approach to garner traction with the opportunity?

4. What exactly happens in each of our meetings with clients and prospects? What are the typical outcomes from each meeting along the way? Do we like the process we've been following? Is it serving our needs?

5. Is there a pattern to our hunting, courting, and closing process from meeting one to meeting number _____?

6. Is there a standard number of meetings, conference calls, site visits, and web-x demonstrations/presentations before we see real traction with the opportunity?

These are great questions to begin with. Our experience suggests that when clients bring together the right people and address these questions, they are surprised by what they learn from one another. They also hear answers they don't like and others they didn't know. For example, without fail, the senior executives think their sales organization is following the sales process that's been put in place by themselves or their predecessors. However, they often come to learn there's plenty more "gray area" around what the salespeople are doing in each meeting. Therefore, these questions and the respective answers bring more clarity. The positive outcome is an open dialogue begins among those who have a stake in the forward progress and top-line growth of the business.

One tool you can use to gain greater clarity around what's actually happening with your current selling and courting process is the Block and Tackle Matrix. Ask your group the following questions and whiteboard the collective responses. Doing this exercise helps companies create a more accurate picture of procedures or processes they may want to change, reorder, or eliminate.

THE BLOCK AND TACKLE MATRIX

(Fill out one for each category)

IN CONFERENCE CALL, IN PERSON, OR MEETING #	HOW MANY PEOPLE ARE TYPICALLY IN ATTENDANCE?	WHAT ARE THE TITLES OF THOSE IN THE ROOM OR INVOLVED?	WHAT IS THE MESSAGE COMMUNICATED? WHAT IS ACTUALLY TAKING PLACE?	WHAT IS THE TYPICAL RESULT OF THE MEETING OR INTERACTION?
1				
2				
3				
4				
5				
6				
7				
8				
9				
10				
11				
12				

We encourage clients to fill in this matrix at least twice—once around how things work now and once around how they'd like them to work going forward. This approach can help DESIGN YOUR FUTURE business hunting and gathering process.

If you wish to take the exercise further you can, by completing a current versus future view around each of the following categories:

1. Current clients

2. Industry verticals you wish to apply more focus to

3. In-progress opportunities that have stalled or gone silent

4. Targeted prospects that appear to be worth hunting

5. Opportunities lost during the last six months

The Block and Tackle Matrix is a useful tool, so let the dialogue within your company begin, and start DESIGNING YOUR FUTURE.

This is a primary tool our clients have used successfully to think through scenarios to compress their closing cycles and time to a deal. The process can feel challenging at times because the answers to the questions, which appear pretty basic, are actually hard to find or see in some cases. Remain open to changing your personal paradigms as you move through the exercise. This will help your business even more.

Here's what I've observed while running training and consulting sessions with anywhere from ten- to fifty-million-dollar companies to multibillion-dollar multinationals that put key people in one room and task them to collaboratively work through the Block and Tackle Matrix:

First, clients who put the right people in the room for this exercise get the most from it. I've already said it once, but it is important enough to mention this list again:

1. The owner, president/CEO, or business unit head

2. The head of sales/business development

3. The head of marketing

4. Two, three, or four key regional or territory vice presidents over the sales managers and producers/client account managers

5. Two, three, or four of the key sales managers/client account managers

6. Two, three, or four top salespeople for the company

7. The chief financial officer for the company/business unit

With such a formidable group in the same room, the strength, experience, and credibility of the facilitator becomes important. The facilitator should be capable of channeling and policing the conversation as things unfold. There's usually plenty of debate, strong opinions, disagreements, and in some cases, heated exchanges. As long as the facilitator keeps everyone focused on the objective of finding tangible ideas that allow the company to tighten and shorten their sales process, then everyone will keep in mind that this work is for a common cause.

This is supposed to be a fun exercise. Any time you get sharp, successful, opinionated people together in one room and task them to explore with this exercise how their current process supposedly works and then to look for ways to improve it, how could you not expect anything but a spirited debate?

As the facilitator helps the group capture their answers on the grid about the first three prospect or client meetings/calls in their current process, things typically hit a snag. In many cases, the salespeople share that, around meeting number three or four, it is impossible for them to nail down exactly the number of people involved or their titles because, as they say, "It just depends." It depends on so many other factors, they insist. This response eventually irritates the management who are present, and they typically respond, *"What do you mean, it depends? How long have we all been doing this? Jeez. I thought we had this stuff all nailed down. This is* basic *block-and-tackle stuff. Let's keep going. We need to flesh this stuff out."*

This tone from management often puts the salespeople on their heels and into a defensive state, because they don't like being "pinned down" to specifics. And they do feel genuinely frustrated with the expectation in the room, when, in their opinion and first-hand experience, it truly does depend.

If you run into this speed bump, here's a suggestion. Flesh out what I call side roads. Define each possible scenario and flesh out each road to its end, to the signing of a deal. In each side road, stick to the grid by defining in each step of your current process how many people are typically involved, their titles, what is happening, and who's doing what.

We often build three or four different branches for clients, emanating from this snag. Those who say you simply can't nail this stuff down are taking the easy way out. If you want to understand why it takes longer than you'd like to bring in business, then pay attention to these branches. They will give you answers to your questions.

Regardless of the snags you encounter, keep moving forward until you finish the matrix for your current sales process. Then take a break and study the responses you put into the grid. Look for patterns. Ask questions about how you could compress your own process.

There's humor in this exercise. On more than a few occasions while running this exercise for clients, senior management has sat back, looked at the responses on the matrix, and said something like, *"Holy buckets. I had no idea. We need help if we can't do better than this."*

Now the group should do the exercise again, but this time with the focus around how you'd like your new process to function from now on.

What I have observed over the years is that clients begin to notice that as the meetings and calls progress from meeting one, then two, then three, etc., the titles of the people who become involved get fancier and fancier. So one suggestion is to see if you could reengineer your new process to compress it by at least 20 percent. We've helped clients compress their new process by as much as half, saving them hundreds of thousands, sometimes millions of dollars in selling expenses. This is why the exercise is valuable and worth your time and attention to conduct. How much money would you save if you could find a way, which everyone buys off on, to shorten/compress your sales process?

Be rigorous with this exercise and keep an open mind. This matrix has opened the eyes of more than a few companies, helping them clean out their pipes and compress their time to a deal. In the words of a Nike campaign, "Just do it."

THIRD ACCELERANT PRINCIPLE
CHARTER YOUR COURSE

YOU HAVE ASSESSED YOUR STATUS, SO YOU KNOW WHICH CONSTRAINTS are slowing your growth. You're either fixing them yourself or getting the help you need to minimize or eliminate them. And you've DESIGNED YOUR FUTURE business hunting process by doing the Block and Tackle Matrix exercise at least twice with your key people, so you all have a clearer focus on what needs to be accomplished at each step of your new process in order to drive the additional revenue growth desired. This exercise will minimize the number of surprises in the sales funnel.

Now you are ready to CHARTER YOUR COURSE toward opportunities you wish to hunt by reviewing your existing client base to determine which clients warrant additional focus and resources. The same applies for key prospects that appear lucrative. I also recommend reviewing your vertical industry attack plans to create aggressive new, outside-the-box ways of shaking the trees in verticals where perhaps you haven't given it your all.

This Accelerant will also help you make course corrections for opportunities already in the funnel that are dragging or have gone

CHARTER YOUR COURSE

silent. A fresh approach might drive them to the finish line—or out of the funnel to conserve valuable resources.

For example, we had a client, a multibillion-dollar technology firm whose central region in the United States had invested about fourteen months with one of the larger cable companies in the country but was essentially nowhere in terms of traction at an executive level. They needed a fresh approach to create some urgency with the prospect, since this deal represented a multimillion-dollar order for the team. Every time the sales team had asked their day-to-day contacts (at the director level) for an executive-level audience, they were effectively denied. Our client's senior management was getting perturbed with the lack of traction and the cost of the effort. They wanted the deal either closed or pushed out of the funnel.

So we were called in like a SWAT team to apply this Accelerant and others to this opportunity and help them bring the deal to fruition. By having the client team review the details of what had taken place during the span of more than a year, we chartered a fresh new approach, which gave them a much tighter value proposition that spoke to the top five senior executives. We then taught them how to use the fifth principle to ACCESS THE CASTLE of this large cable concern. Lo and behold, my client got their day in the sun with a few of the EVPs in one room, for about thirty to forty-five minutes—long enough to expand upon the message mentioned in their approach letter. The Accelerants can help you think outside the box to create fresh approaches to deals falling silent, or stalled, as this one was.

If you are still reeling from opportunities you didn't win, doesn't it make sense to CHARTER YOUR COURSE for the ones lost during the last six months, once you learn how all the Accelerants work together? Wouldn't closing one of those opportunities be worth the effort?

CHARTERING YOUR COURSE around the five categories listed in Accelerant principle two, DESIGN YOUR FUTURE, is as easy as going to the nearest whiteboard, not answering the phone for a day or so, and chartering your strategy to gain more business in each of these five areas such as with existing clients, new prospects, etc. It doesn't need to be a long, drawn-out exercise. In fact, thinking through where to apply additional focus and resources to gain additional business is invigorating.

Some liken this Accelerant to their strategic account planning and review procedure, and in one sense, it can be thought of in this vein. After you read about Accelerants four and five, you may want to emulate what we often do with clients—bring them back to this third Accelerant, showing them how to "group" certain competing companies they want to hunt (based on revenues) in each of the five categories into Accelerant Campaigns, such that certain companies are approached simultaneously—something called an Accelerant Blitz. In Section Three, the last two Success Stories will give you real-life examples of the power and additional impact clients gain when using the Accelerant Blitz tool set. This is one way to maximize the power, efficiencies, and "punch" the Accelerants pack, creating even more urgency for the prospect or client to act on your offer/message.

CHARTER YOUR COURSE by identifying the companies you want to focus your time and energy on. This will help your company feel more organized, and everyone involved in your business-gathering efforts will know where to focus their energy.

METRIC THE MESSAGE

*B*ELOW ARE SEVEN SETS OF VALUE PROPOSITIONS. I USED THE FIRST one in my technology business, primarily on large and mid-sized corporations. The second was part of a value proposition used by a client—a five-hundred-million-dollar-plus technology services firm that competes with EDS, IBM, CSC, Accenture, and other multibillion-dollar multinationals. Research In Motion used the third message years ago as a part of their value proposition in marketing their amazingly successful BlackBerry handheld device. The remaining value propositions give you additional examples of what messages in other industries could sound like if you happen to be in those businesses. Each set represents a different product or service offering. Read each set and determine which statements (A or B) do a better job of drawing your attention and piquing your interest.

Set One

A: "Our predictive-dialing solution can improve the productivity (talk time per hour) of your collections department because the collectors can reach more debtors during the same shift."

METRIC THE MESSAGE

B: "Our predictive-dialing solution can improve the talk time per hour of each collector in your collections department. We estimate it currently is eighteen to twenty-four minutes per hour, and our solution could increase it to as much as forty-five minutes each hour. This could nearly double your collectors' productivity—either increasing the dollars collected without increasing your labor expense or maintaining your current level of collections while reducing your labor and health-care expenses in the range of 35 to 45 percent. The choice is yours."

Set Two

A: "Our organization has been able to help clients reduce the amount they spend annually to maintain their existing legacy IT applications."

B: "Our organization has been able to help certain clients reduce the amount they spend annually to maintain their existing legacy IT applications by 5 to 15 percent."

Set Three

A: "Our wireless, mobile, handheld device can help increase the productivity levels of your field sales and customer support professionals each and every day."

B: "Our wireless, mobile, handheld device could 'find' an extra thirty to sixty minutes of additional time every day for each one of your field sales and customer support professionals. We believe this extra time could enhance their overall productivity levels in the range of 5 to 10 percent."

Set Four

A: "Clients who have implemented our recognition and rewards programs have seen an increase in the sales performance of their sales and business development organization."

B: "Clients who have implemented our recognition and rewards programs have seen a 2 to 5 percent increase in the annual sales performance of their sales and business development organization. What would that level of increase mean for your company?"

Set Five

A: "Our line of granola cereals has, on average, less sugar than other leading granola brands, providing your customers with a much healthier choice."

B: "Our line of granola cereals has, on average, 25 percent less sugar than any other leading granola brand on the market, providing your customers with a much healthier choice."

Set Six

A: "During my thirty years as a Certified Financial Planner, I have helped my clients attain their unique financial and retirement goals."

B: "During my thirty years as a Certified Financial Planner, I have helped my clients attain their unique financial and retirement goals one to three years earlier than they had originally planned."

Set Seven

A: "As a successful residential Realtor with more than ten years in the business, I specialize in assisting buyers and sellers in maximizing their objectives when it comes to lake-home living in the western suburbs of Minneapolis."

B: "As a successful residential Realtor with more than ten years in the business, I specialize in assisting buyers and sellers in maximizing their objectives when it comes to lake-home living in the western suburbs of Minneapolis. To be more specific, in calendar 2005, of all Realtors who specialize in the Lake Minnetonka and surrounding area, I was ranked number three in selling properties for more than $1,000,000."

METRIC THE MESSAGE. I think you see where this Accelerant is heading. Who is asking you to metric your message? Global competitive trends, prospects, and your clients. This should be reason enough to take this Accelerant principle seriously.

If you want to lead, you must METRIC THE MESSAGE, regardless of your business, the position you hold, the industry sectors you serve, whether your company is a market leader, or whatever you market—a product, service, solution, or concept. Today, every organization should have a well-defined, clear, crisp value proposition containing some form of metric (if possible) for each product, service, solution, or cause they represent.

Because of the perceived commoditization of many companies' offerings, prospects and clients often believe they can get about the same thing from at least two other providers as they can from you. Regardless of whether it is true, they perceive it to be the case. And in this way they exert leverage over your firm. Sometimes this shows itself in their belief that they don't *need* to see anyone from your company initially, if ever. Instead, they prefer to learn about your company's offerings through your Web site, the Internet, or any collateral you can forward to them.

Think about times in the last month when you've pushed a client or prospect pretty aggressively for a meeting, and they've said something like, *"That's OK. I appreciate your interest in meeting, and at some point we probably need to do that. But at this time, I think it's premature. Why don't you send the information you'd like us to review, follow up with me in two or three weeks, and we'll take it from there, all right?"*

Clients and prospects may view your company's offerings as interchangeable with your competition's. This ought to motivate you to revisit the value propositions of your offerings to ensure they are condensed, compelling, easily understood, and contain some form of financial metric that describes the approximate value or outcome your offerings could produce. That way, you will be able to present your offerings as frequently as needed to achieve your revenue objectives.

Based on what I've experienced from years of delivering these training programs and consulting sessions, many organizations are in *denial* about needing to improve their value propositions by putting financial metrics inside their messages. Their attitude has been, *"Let's get in the door first and draw the client or prospect out, then they'll tell us what they're looking to do. So I don't see the need to sharpen our messages, when they're going to tell us what's important to them anyway."*

Given the nature of how competitive things have become in almost every industry, this line of thinking is *a terrible mistake.* It is a lazy attitude that will negatively impact your closing cycles and cost of sales by lengthening your time to a deal. Without clearly defining the metric benefits or outcomes your offerings could drive, you won't be able to access the people who have the power to make things happen as fast as you want. Elegant-sounding value propositions without any metrics are one of the primary reasons why you might not be getting the "power audiences" you want and need to close more business in a shorter time frame.

As their choices increase, it becomes *much* more difficult for prospects and clients to discern any real differences between available providers. When this happens, they begin looking for substance among all provider claims. Senior executives and owners call it the TEETH, or financial metrics.

Because clients are having an increasingly difficult time deciphering the benefits of one alternative over another, they will often select the option they can most easily justify to "the powers that be" within their company. That means they will look first for the TEETH. If these are not present in the message, they will not ask why. Instead, they will bypass your option and move to those companies that offer some type of metric. They want to be able to compare available options more easily, drilling down if necessary so they can make a decision.

The people you want to approach on an ongoing basis are putting more stock and credibility in providers who take the time to figure out and then explain in a cohesive and articulate fashion the metrics of their solution. Many organizations struggle in this area because it can be a challenge to gain agreement within the organization as to what the TEETH are for each of their offerings.

Metrics in your value propositions become even more critical for gaining executive-level access or exposure to an existing client or prospect. That's because money is foremost on their minds in the executive suite. They want to understand quickly if or how your offering could positively impact stock price, debt levels, client satisfaction ratings, government standards, market share, margin and profit ratios, quality standards, client retention levels, agility or streamlining, and reduction of legal exposure. The list could go on and on. The key is to articulate how much your offer could impact any of these factors, and if so, by what range? Since vendor-providers typically won't *lead* with this type of value proposition (because they feel they don't need to), those who do often find themselves first to be invited to present their offerings—another reason why you should discuss the importance of this Accelerant with colleagues.

Over years of running value proposition-training and management-consulting sessions with senior management, we've developed a methodology that has helped small, midsized, and multinational clients develop enterprisewide messages at the parent organization level for companies that have multiple business units. These messages articulate the financial benefits of doing business with them at an enterprisewide level. This has been extremely beneficial in helping clients do larger, multiyear deals that include products and services from several or all of their business units. This style of selling "big deals" also delights the procurement departments of your clients, because they can enjoy even greater economies of scale. In addition, you, the provider, have an even better chance of pulling in the very top people, simply because the deals warrant that much more attention from the top.

The same methodology for condensing and articulating the metrics that should go inside your retuned value propositions also applies at the business-unit level. This proven process can improve, tighten, and articulate the messages around the core offerings for each of your business units.

Here is an example of an enterprisewide-level value proposition that we helped create for one of our technology clients—a firm with more than five hundred million dollars in annual revenues and a respected player for more than twenty years. They used this message very effectively. Notice it's wordy and doesn't speak directly to any specific product, service, or solution. Instead, it encapsulates (in high-level, "layman" terms, which top officers understand) several of their offerings, cascading this message to the highest levels of targeted companies, helping drive larger deals in a shorter time horizon. Here's their value proposition:

If you engage in a business relationship with our organization, we can, through our capabilities, skill sets, experience, and more than forty different offerings, help you:

1. Strip between 5 to 15 percent out of the amount of money currently being spent annually on maintaining your existing legacy IT applications.

2. Improve the quality of existing legacy applications service levels by 10 percent per year.

3. Take this newfound "chunk" of capital we have just "freed up," and redeploy it, by helping you create, implement, and manage your own e-commerce road map, giving you e-commerce solutions and customer-facing IT processes that will help your business become leaner, faster, more flexible, and more profitable.

Said in plain English, *"Without another dime spent on your total IT budget, we will find—within your existing IT annual budget— between X and Y million dollars and help you reinvest these dollars into e-commerce solutions that will give you more control, so that you can drive your business to be leaner, faster, more flexible, and more profitable."*

Imagine being the recipient of this message. You could grab your calculator, make some estimates as to the financial impact this message could have for your company—low-side, high-side—and make a relatively quick decision as to whether you'd like to visit with them. And this is *exactly* what can happen when top officers receive this kind of enterprisewide-level value proposition. It does pull more attention in many instances. The hard part is to nail down the message first. This is what you need to focus on if you expect to do larger deals in a shorter time horizon. Your work on the front end will pay off if your value propositions turn out to have some real TEETH that you can back up.

This type of message causes more discussion among the senior ranks of prospects and clients because at the end of the day, it is all about the money—something they *all* have in common. The recipients may not necessarily *believe* your message, but in one sense, that's not the point; it helps get your message discussed and debated with the people you elect to target. Notice that the messages aren't about the features and benefits of your offerings, which is the way we've all been taught to sell.

This type of enterprisewide message can be generated regardless of the business you are in: hospitality, travel, meetings and incentives, manufacturing, financial services, medical devices, technology, management services, accounting and internal audit, etc. We have helped companies in the staffing, technology, telecommunications, financial services, and other sectors create messages that generate more urgency with key executives in targeted companies.

There is another big trend that will become even more pronounced in the years ahead. I've alluded to it already: The large companies you serve are *demanding* that providers streamline their sales operations and reduce the amount of sales divisions/people that call on them. They are voicing their discontent with being "pummeled" by each division's sales teams and want that number reduced.

Basically, they are asking that providers do a better job of selling more or *all* of their offerings with fewer salespeople. They want those who do call on them to be able to speak intelligently about *all* that the company has to offer. *Guess what?* This is a very strong signal from your clients that they want you selling to them in an enterprisewide manner. This is why financially crafted value propositions are becoming more and more necessary for your sustained revenue growth and success.

METRIC THE MESSAGE. Help prospects and clients understand easily and quickly why your offerings are a better choice than the alternatives by communicating the financial outcomes your offerings could deliver.

We offer assistance in this area through executive workshops, training programs, and consulting guidance. For more information, please see the back of the book.

ACCESS THE CASTLE

YOU HAVE ASSESSED YOUR STATUS, DESIGNED YOUR FUTURE, CHARTERED YOUR COURSE, and METRICED YOUR MESSAGE(S) at an enterprisewide level and for each business unit's core offerings. Clients who implement these Accelerants experience a general excitement within their organizations because their level of preparedness is higher than normal. They are ready for the next step and believe they can "take any castle!" This Accelerant helps your company more effectively approach prospect and client opportunities on the course you have chartered for your business—collapsing your time to a deal.

The fifth Accelerant is 100 percent about *access*. It's about using a direct, honest and ethical, field-proven, psychologically sound methodology for getting a meeting, conference call, video conference, e-mail conversation, or any other kind of access with the decision makers. It is a best practice tool set that takes the work you've done in the first four Accelerants and gives you a road map to more efficiently get with those decision makers who can pull the trigger on your offerings if they like your value propositions. This step-by-step system can give you faster, more effective access to the people you want and need exposure to, so you have the opportunity to do more business. You can't hit a single, double, triple, or a *home run,* if you can't get up to bat. This Accelerant will give you more *at bats* with the audience of decision makers you desire.

Given the business climate in most industry sectors, most clients report that getting access to the right decision makers has gradually become tougher and takes longer than it ever has. And with deals they've lost, clients often believe it was because they didn't have "their arms around" the key decision makers.

It's usually not that difficult, if you're the CEO or other top executive, to get access at the levels you desire. You have the power, title, and authority to pick up the phone and make it happen. But that is *not* the way it is for your people. *Not at all.* They don't carry the same title or level of command and control. So unless you plan on making *all* the introductions for *all* of your business developers, please heed this Accelerant because it works.

Many of our clients spend a lot of time with people who claim they are the decision makers, only to learn later in the game that at best, these people are glorified recommenders. The real decision makers are usually higher in the company, behind numerous executive assistants, handlers, and blockers. This Accelerant has helped our clients, and hundreds of other companies, to make that direct connection faster.

No matter what business you are in, there's no doubt you want your best shot at being heard and considered by the appropriate powers that be. In fact, every client that goes through our training programs on this Accelerant holds the belief *"If we could just get in higher, to the people we prefer to be in front of, earlier on in our process, we could assess and close business faster and save money on our cost of sales at the same time."*

One problem that impedes revenue growth, slowing a company's time to a deal, is entering too low in target companies they wish to garner traction with. The reason they are too low is because the individuals with the power, authority, and budget control have relocated to a different part of the company—typically higher. But your sales force has yet to make the adjustment.

If you review the Block and Tackle Matrix for how you'd like your new approach process to work, where are your decision makers located? Exactly where in the castle are they hiding? Does it make good business sense to call on these individuals last? What if you never make it to that point? What type of audience do you need to be in front of to increase the probabilities of closing in less time?

Review your debate on the seventh and eighth constraints (Your Level of Engagement, and The Inability to Articulate Your Value Proposition to the Real Decision Makers) with others in your company. Your decisions about where you elect to enter a target organization—and with what message—are critical to your ability to reduce your time to a deal. These decisions must be well thought through. It boils down to the speed at which you wish to attempt to close opportunities. This is why the Block and Tackle Matrix is so useful with helping you analyze which executives you should be targeting in your effort to compress your closing cycle(s).

It's not appropriate to go right to the top all the time because it depends on the stage of the courting process. However, there is evidence suggesting that if you want to get something done faster—go to the top.

Now relax. ACCESSING THE CASTLE is not the appropriate solution to all approach needs. Clearly, the referral approach is a tried-and-true method for getting in to see people, even though it doesn't work all the time, either. The referral approach can also take a long time and be somewhat expensive. And though a referral gets you an audience in many cases, is it the right audience? Is it the audience that will help you navigate inside the maze of people and divisions, properly representing your message, or could your referral lead you down a dead end? According to what we hear from clients, this happens more frequently than they'd like to admit.

Successful companies identify multiple paths they can take and are prepared for multiple scenarios. Think of ACCESSING THE CASTLE as one powerful method—another tool to use when the need presents itself and you want action. Remember, if it's action you want, go where the action usually is—typically at least halfway up the castle, if not near or at the top.

ACCESSING THE CASTLE refers to a field-proven process called the Circle of Leverage System—or COL. This best-practice methodology helps to more quickly and effectively gain access to the individual or group you desire an audience with. It has yielded amazing results for organizations that have used it, often becoming their preferred standard for gaining access to prospects and clients. We provide training programs on this system, because the process should be designed and calibrated properly to the target audience(s), based on the provider's product, service, or solution, and the enterprisewide or business-unit value propositions they wish to put forth.

Here are the underlying premises behind the Circle of Leverage System:

1. On any given day, prospects and clients are not interested in granting access (an appointment, conference call, web-x, or video conference) so they can learn more about how your product, service, or solution offering might help them and their organization.

2. In today's business world, approaching one individual at a time within any company has become much less effective and often a waste of time for the prospector. This is because decisions are often

not made by one individual, regardless of what is represented. Decisions are made via groups, teams, committees, or task forces. This has become the new norm. Therefore, approaching a few carefully selected individuals at one time has proven to be more effective, productive, cost efficient (for both sides)—and consistent with the commonly accepted decision-making processes of most organizations, large and small.

3. The net benefits of the product, service, or solution (regardless of how legitimate they may be) rarely provide enough urgency or incentive anymore for prospects and clients to grant access so they can listen to your presentation. Their power of choice is too great and their level of trust usually quiet low.

4. Finding and gaining access to more than one internal champion, executive sponsor, or coach earlier on in the courting process actually helps the prospect or client make decisions with a higher level of comfort—increasing the probability of closing more business and reducing your closing cycles and cost of sales.

5. Doing homework or background research on the entity you wish to approach (if only fifteen minutes' worth), instead of getting the appointment and expecting the prospect to educate you about their business, helps target opportunities more effectively. It is also a more respectful approach, garnering more credibility and rapport with prospects and clients.

6. A strong level of confidence in your product or service offering is required. You must feel your offerings are worthy of the right audience's time and attention.

In summary, the COL System is a planned approach for simultaneously putting your value proposition(s) in front of the multiple individuals you've selected. You do this via a letter, voice mail, or e-mail, "broadcasting" the value propositions of your product or service—asking for their guidance and assistance in granting an audience with them—or being directed to the person(s) they feel are the "appropriate" individuals to hear your pitch.

Often, the individuals you appeal to have their own agendas on top of the company's agenda, though they all work for the same company. Therefore, each person may respond differently to the value propositions you describe. Hence, they often *can't decide* as a group who the most appropriate person or people are to handle the request for an appointment.

This internal discussion and debate is *designed* to take place and is part of how the COL System works. If you think about it, what are they discussing and debating? The value propositions you have put before them. This process not only helps you gain access faster, but it can increase the number of people in your meetings, which is a good thing, since most organizations make decisions in groups or teams.

Here's an example of a client who used the COL System to not only simultaneously get access to several multibillion-dollar oil companies but also to elevate their level of conversations to the executive suite—five to six levels *above* where they typically "land" inside multinational prospects.

The client was a small, privately held document-processing firm with under ten million in revenue. Their niche: scanning, imaging, and storing the electronic documents at issue for companies involved in large-scale litigation. This meant they typically targeted large corporations with several layers of decision makers and recommenders.

When I was hired, they were getting about one dollar per page for their services, so targeting a company with ten million documents at issue was a ten-million-dollar opportunity.

Intense competition in the industry fostered a commodity perception by the big buyers of these services. Their attitude was that these vendors were "a dime a dozen." As a result, this firm was typically relegated to dealing with a low-level assistant to an assistant, to the assistant vice president and associate general counsel, or with that person's equivalent with the prospect's outside counsel. They were used to getting kicked around inside client and prospect companies.

A portion of the COL System letter template you will read shortly was designed and calibrated to "land" our client in the general counsel's office of these huge petroleum conglomerates, creating enough interest and urgency to secure a thirty-minute face-to-face meeting with that person. This would enable them to present their offering and hopefully earn the right to bid on a current or future project.

The following is a portion of their COL letter template. Notice how different it is from the standard business letter we have all been taught to write. This letter was sent (via regular U.S. first-class mail) to five senior executives inside each targeted U.S. multibillion-dollar oil company: the CEO/president, the CFO, the VP of finance, the general counsel, and the associate general counsel in charge of litigation.

In some cases, our client was targeting up to five oil companies simultaneously with this system as part of an Accelerant Campaign Blitz. This approach helped create even more urgency to respond. Here are the first two sections of the letter, which was sent to the following people, whose names are fictitious:

The CEO and president—Bob Jones
The CFO—Mary Thompson–Lee
The VP of finance—Kathleen Van Patten
The general counsel—Michael Stevens
The associate general counsel/litigation—Deborah Roth

Dear Mr. Jones,

You do not know me, nor do we have any credibility with you or any current business relationship with your organization, even though we are currently providing our services to organizations of your size, such as _____, _____, and _____.

Nowadays, because most important decisions within corporations are typically analyzed and made in groups, I am writing to you, Mary Thompson-Lee, Kathleen Van Patten, Michael Stevens, and Deborah Roth to learn from the five of you who you think are the most appropriate senior people we should deal with in regard to scheduling a thirty-minute, in-person presentation within the next two to three weeks to share how our organization could help you do three things:

1. Reduce your total cost of scanning, imaging, and storing all documents at issue in currently active or upcoming litigation-related matters for 10 percent less than you currently spend;

2. Maintain the same speed, quality, document integrity, and on-site capabilities you currently enjoy; and

3. Provide a secure, central repository for the documents for all in-house and out-of-house counsel needing access to the document population.

This was the opening section of the letter, which articulated the TEETH within the firm's value proposition right away. The five senior people receiving the letter don't know who you'd like to meet with, because you didn't say. Instead, it asks them who they think is most appropriate to handle this potential meeting. First, this type of request causes discussion among them, because they can't always agree on who should handle it. Secondly, they are discussing *your value proposition* and whether they feel they need it, or have any interest at all. Therefore, this approach creates more discussion, debate, and sometimes disagreement among those you've targeted. This is a good thing, because as your letter is bouncing around, each recipient is debating whether or not a meeting is necessary or desired, and if so, who should be tasked to handle it.

Now, a word of caution. The COL System is a psychologically steeped process involving a specific follow-up component, which is why clients get the training—so they can customize the process around their core offerings and targeted clients and prospects.

Suffice it to say, the COL System delivered several meetings (a 50 percent hit rate) with the general counsel's office within huge oil companies—executives who typically do not meet with document-processing vendors because they view it as not really worthy of their time. Someone much lower in the organization typically handles it. However, because the message in the letter offered concrete financial value, our client was able to close some nice business fairly rapidly, in comparison to their standard approach process, pre-COL. This was because the *primary* decision maker—the person with the power, authority, and control over budget to make it happen—was present.

Please remember that this is a small portion of what a complete COL letter can look like. There are numerous versions that can be used depending on the client's objectives. Therefore, my coaching is not to get ahead of yourself and think this Accelerant is some neat little letter-writing "trick." The reason we have a three-day training program around this Accelerant—and the reason several Fortune 500 companies have invested real dollars in sending their producers to learn the process—is because it is an advanced best-practice tool set that carries a deep, psychologically sound philosophy about what drives people to *want* to see you. We teach the process and show clients how to use the tool, based on the companies and the levels of executives they want more access and exposure to. The fact that this proven tool set has given me access to Bill Gates and other CEOs of Fortune 1000 organizations should indicate the precision power this Accelerant packs.

There are numerous variations and levels of strength around using the COL System as an effective approach strategy for the myriad prospects, current clients, and in-progress scenarios. This is precisely why we offer three levels of training on this approach process for those serious about wanting to compress their closing cycles. You will learn about various versions of COL matrixes designed to accomplish different challenges related to gaining access and exposure to the desired audiences. Each matrix can be dialed and customized to the objectives of the user, based on the situation at hand. This will increase the probability of being heard by the right individuals. Vertical industry campaigns and COL blitzes on targeted opportunities where a handful of companies are approached simultaneously are examples of different scenarios in which the COL System can be very effective. Each application has a COL matrix—essentially, a specific pattern in which the methodology can be tailored for maximum impact.

Thousands of individuals also use the COL System to find a new or different job. It is a superb tool by itself or in concert with an online or executive search firm option. It is also useful in accessing difficult-to-reach people, such as well-known doctors, media people, politicians, board members, etc.

For more information on the training programs around this Accelerant, visit www.accelerantinternational.com.

ACCELERANT SUCCESS STORY:
ROCK-SOLID REFERRALS DON'T ALWAYS ROCK—OR ROLL

During the early years of our training and consulting company, I was hungry for some business in the insurance industry, especially the big life, property, and casualty insurers. Never having prospected that industry, I went to one of my mentors, the chairman of North American Life, one of the large insurance companies in the Twin Cities at that time, now part of Allianz.

I presented my story and asked if he would be willing (since he was an advocate for the COL System) to introduce me or give me a referral or two to some of his peers who run other insurance companies throughout the country. (His firm was not a prospect because of how they sold their lines of insurance.)

Because of the relationship we had developed over many years, he said he would refer me to the chairman of The Equitable Life Insurance Company of America (now AXA Equitable), headquartered in New York. He said they respected each other, and that he'd write a letter urging him to consider looking into how I could provide our "access training program" to their five thousand-plus field salespeople nationwide.

Fantastic! I of course accepted. My mentor wrote the letter to the chairman of The Equitable, urging him to take my call to discuss how we could provide his organization value by shrinking their time to a deal by helping their producers get with the key decision makers they were targeting faster, and more effectively.

So out went the letter. His executive assistant called to inform me that it should land in New York on "x" date, and that I should follow up within a week or so. *Perfect,* I thought. No need for my own tools to get in the door with The Equitable. I am going to be speaking with the chairman and CEO of one of the largest life providers in the nation. *So,* I put my "tools" in my pocket and didn't bother with my own methodology—my own proven system to get access, because I basically didn't need it, right? I mean, what for? I was going to use one of the oldest, most effective, and most accepted forms of getting an introduction that there is on the planet—the good old, trustworthy *referral.* And this was no ordinary referral, but one between two peers who compete in the same industry but respect each other as well.

I thought this was bulletproof. I'd have my opportunity to persuade the chairman, even if for a brief few minutes, and if he was intrigued, maybe I'd be passed down to one of his key people so that I could have the opportunity to at least present my offerings in person at a later date, and get a relatively fast answer on whether they were open to an initial program or two as a test pilot.

Perfect—Perfect—Perfect. I followed up the letter as directed, but was quickly "routed" down by one of his executive assistants to a very low-level person in Equitable University—the training and educational unit of the company, run in a different city. I asked the assistant if the chairman had seen the letter, which I referenced for her, and would he be open to speaking for a few minutes—or if he was not in, would it be possible to set up a five-minute conference call with him to discuss the letter received from the chairman of North American Life in Minneapolis? I didn't really get a straight answer. I suspect the CEO never *saw* the letter, but somehow it was internally routed by the CEO's assistant to *the appropriate person* she felt should handle it or review my offerings.

What a bummer. I never spoke to the chairman, didn't really learn if he saw the letter because I didn't want to press the executive assistant—and all of a sudden, I'd been routed to another city, to a low-level "somebody," being told effectively that the chairman was not the correct place to start. In most cases, I would certainly agree. But this was not your typical case. I had had a direct, personal *referral*. I was not expecting the brush-off.

I did what I was told, following up with the individual it was routed to, and was basically shut down and blown off. Even with a referral from one chairman of the board to another I was basically *blocked*—intentionally or not, I will never know—by his executive assistants. Has this ever happened to you?

A confusing, and sometimes irritating occurrence, isn't it? Right or wrong, I told my mentor about not getting through and being routed down to an area where I didn't want to go, seeing if he'd pick up the phone and call Joe. But no such luck. He felt, "If that's where they want you to start, then that's where you need to start."

Now what? I decided to wait about six months and give it a go again. But this time, I'd use my own COL System to see if I could get any traction at the top of one of the largest and most respected insurance companies in the country.

I crafted my COL letter to five senior executives at The Equitable: the chairman, the CFO, the EVP, SVP, and VP of sales/agency operations worldwide, informing them that about six months earlier I had been referred by the chairman of North American Life in Minneapolis, to the chairman of the Equitable, because he thought our offerings were worthy of a look-see to potentially benefit their sizeable field force in producing even more business.

In classic pattern-specific form, upon follow-up with the chairman's office, I was told he had seen the letter, that it had been routed to his direct report, the EVP and chief agency officer, to handle, and that I should follow up with him, per the chairman's direction. I did so, but not before I first followed up with the executive assistant to the CFO to learn if he had seen his letter and whether he was interested in scheduling a five-minute conference call. From his executive assistant, I learned he had also routed his letter over to the EVP and chief agency officer—who now had three of the letters: the chairman's, the CFO's, and the one I sent him directly.

Upon follow-up with the EVP's executive assistant, I learned he was aware of the letter, had read it, and routed it to be handled by one of his direct reports, the VP and chief agency officer—who now had two letters: the EVP's and the one that was sent him directly. (A lot of work in follow-up? Not for the result it produced, for the cost of writing one letter tailored to five executives, all sent out at the same time, via five, thirty-nine-cent postage stamps.)

I followed up with the executive assistant to the VP and was told that he wanted to book an in-person appointment for me to come to New York and present my capabilities for an initial determination as to whether I should be sent to the head of Equitable University's senior management for further review.

Within thirty days, I was in New York at the headquarters of Equitable Life Insurance presenting my offerings to basically the second guy in charge of the entire field force. Not a bad result for the COL. Unfortunately, I did not close any business there, because ultimately they thought my services were not needed.

The key point is this: Whether they needed our services or not I had access at a very high level. And with that, I could navigate my way to a close much faster than any of my competitors who were talking to a mid- to low-level contact inside Equitable University. At that rate it would take twelve to eighteen months in courting expense, time, and effort to get to the level at which I had begun. Instead, I stepped it up a notch by using the COL System and ACCESS THE CASTLE in a professional, respectful manner. Even though I didn't get the order, I was shown again the power and effectiveness of this Accelerant.

DELIVER THE ULTIMATE PRESENTATION

*Y*OU'VE WORKED HARD TO GET IN FRONT OF THE RIGHT AUDIENCE OF decision makers—people with short attention spans and enormous pressure to deal with. Don't risk blowing the entire meeting by asking one of those fabulously brilliant questions we've all been trained to ask, like *"What keeps you up at night, Bob?"* What if they're not in the mood to open up to you? And is it smart to go through the twenty, thirty, or forty-plus slides in your boilerplate PowerPoint presentation, expecting them to be intrigued? This Accelerant will teach you about a field-proven tool called the 1/3rd . . . 2/3rds Condensed Presentation Format. This way of presenting will impress and knock the socks off everyone in your audience because they'll enjoy your presentation more (and so will you). Perhaps more important, it will give you added control and leverage. This format plays perfectly to the high levels of decision makers you will now have in front of you more frequently, thanks to Accelerants one through five.

To understand the power and simplicity of this Accelerant, it's best to look at this skill set through the eyes of the client or prospect

first. By putting yourself in their world and visualizing what it's like to sit through one of your standard dog and pony shows, you may get some fast answers about what could be changed or reordered to enhance their experience. So let's do it—let's walk in their shoes.

You've just received an e-mail from your boss asking you and two of your peers to attend a thirty-minute presentation on Friday at 2 P.M. You've never heard of the company that's giving the presentation, so they must be trying to get your business. You check your calendar, hoping you have a conflict so you can gracefully back out, but lo and behold you have no conflicts.

Friday arrives and you've already been on the job since 7 A.M. The day is crazy and you are stressed. Things have gotten all jumbled up and nothing is flowing smoothly—then there's that presentation at 2 P.M. You send an e-mail to your colleagues to see if they are still planning to attend, hoping they can cover for you or suggest you really don't need to be there. But it was your *boss* who asked you to attend, so you decide against pulling anything like that. You hit the company's Web site hoping maybe you've already seen this pitch, but no, it doesn't appear you have.

It's 1:45 P.M. You receive an e-mail from your boss saying that due to a scheduling mix-up the presentation will be moved to conference room C (the one without windows, a dingy paint job, and an air-conditioning system so loud it's hard to hear). You respond to your boss with "I'll be there—looking forward to it."

At 2 P.M. you're sitting around the table in conference room C after introducing yourself to the two people from the vendor company who appear *so excited* to be there, they've had either way too much caffeine or just returned from a high-school pep fest.

And here we go. A thirty-minute presentation, baloney. This will go forty-five minutes for sure, if not longer. The room darkens a bit, so you slouch in your chair, can't see the screen all that well, but it's not important, because you know the first twenty minutes are not that critical, since the meat (pricing, specifics, time frames, and next steps) are all probably toward the end anyway. You decide you'll be pleasant, sitting there with great interest while you dial out for the next fifteen to twenty minutes. Just then, you notice you forgot something to write with. The day is not going well. "And why am I here? Do I really need to be here?" you ask yourself.

Of course this is only a characterization. The point is that you need to grab the attention of prospects and clients who may be tired, bored, distracted, or all of the above. Plus, they already have a perception about what they are about to see, and that the first portion of the presentation is not that important anyway. And here you come with a boilerplate PowerPoint presentation that maybe even you dislike (remember the eleventh constraint). So you can understand why there's often a lack of enthusiasm on the part of recipients about even attending, let alone paying attention to your presentation.

You can learn how to Deliver the Ultimate Presentation by using this best practice called the 1/3rd . . . 2/3rds Condensed Presentation Format. A process of presenting your story in one-third the amount of time you request for your meeting. This will provide ideas that will add value if they were included in your standard presentation.

There is no doubt a general order to the content of a typical presentation. Perhaps the structure looks like this:

1. General Introductions; Thank You for the Opportunity

2. Brief Background on Our Company, Who We Are, How We Help, etc.

3. Brief Background on Our Products, Services, Solutions, etc.

4. The Net Benefits of Our Offerings

5. Partial List of Clients We Serve

6. A Few Client Testimonials and Case Histories

7. How Could We Help Your Company? Needs Assessment, Etc.

8. Mutual Determination of Next Steps

In terms of the style of delivery, it's perhaps delivered via laptop computer, which may be projected onto a wall surface or screen, depending on the number of people in attendance. The presenters might spend a portion of their delivery sitting down, watching the slides on the screen as they move through the content. They may not walk around the room much as they present, if at all. In terms of intonation of their voice, it's probably professional and "even," since nobody wants to be too excited, lest they come across like a circus act.

This is what we have heard from clients of all sizes. We also hear comments regarding how they'd like the presentation ordered if it were given to them. Here is some of their feedback:

"It should be structured like the evening news where, in the first sixty seconds, we receive a quick overview of just the high points, so we know what's going to be covered and can determine if we want to keep watching."

"Why do I need to wait until the end to find out how much, how fast, the time lines, the ROI, the terms, and next steps? As an executive, I'd like to know these things right away, because that is the 'meat' of the presentation. This is what I want to know, the earlier the better, if they expect me to pay attention. Even if it's my own people presenting to me, this is what I want to know right out of the box."

"Make it shorter and snappier. Remove all the 'nice-to-know' stuff because it's often irrelevant to my decision process."

"Give me someone who actually believes what they're presenting. A little enthusiasm would be nice to see now and again."

"I have a harder time seeing things on a laptop. I like to mix it up a

little, like the old chalk talk on game day. Why don't presenters use my whiteboard or the flip charts in our conference rooms more frequently? So what if it's not that high-tech. Who cares? I want to understand the pitch, and if I can visualize it better, I can comprehend it faster."

The 1/3rd . . . 2/3rds Condensed Presentation Format takes into account all this feedback. The net-net of the format is this: Divide the total time you will have for your presentation into thirds. In the first third of that time, your goal is to cover just the high points—the salient aspects of each of the key points in your entire presentation. This means if there were eight different sections or components to the presentation, then you would cover the top third of each of these areas. Once this is complete, you should have "burned" about one third of your allotted meeting time, and two thirds of the time should remain.

You are now done—for the moment. You have covered the first third of each one of your key points in the first third of the allotted time, so you are essentially done until you turn over pseudocontrol to the recipients, asking if they have any questions you can answer before discussing next steps.

Remember, there is two thirds of your allotted time left. This is what you should strive for. At this point, recipients are typically silent and in shock, as everything that needed to be covered has basically been covered in a third of the time they were expecting. Clients and prospects may give you a look as though they are in love with you. They are pleasantly surprised and impressed with the level of organization and time management.

Questions will usually begin to come at this point, so let them ask away. They will bounce all over the map, jumping around among your key points. And if you stop and think, "Who is in control of the room and the presentation at this point, the recipient(s) or the presenter(s)?" It will be the presenter if you've done a good job in the first third. Why? Because as questions come forth, you still have two-thirds more information you can cover on each key point *if the recipients request it*—so recipients feel *they* are in control of the meeting. They are getting their questions answered in the exact order they want.

The careful ordering of content is what makes this format effective (and senior executives invite you to lunch). This will take some deliberation. It will be crucial in your opening statement (before "point one" of the content) to provide the net-net of the messages you wish to drive home with the audience. This becomes the frosting of the presentation and what owners and senior executives love to hear right away—the *teeth.* This type of organization requires thought, but it is worth the end result.

Here is an example of a frosting statement: *"The basic gist of what we'd like to convey today is how—with an investment of approximately 'x' to 'y,' we can, through our capabilities, products, and solutions, reduce your current_____, in the range of 'x' to 'y' percent, over the course of_____months/years. This we believe should provide a payback in the range of_____months/years, and an ROI of 'x'."*

And those charged with decision-making power appreciate the level of brevity, confidence, and precision. As you develop your frosting statement, focus and drill down on your message. The 1/3rd . . . 2/3rds Condensed Presentation Format is an amazingly effective best practice that will help you DELIVER THE ULTIMATE PRESENTATION.

On page 140 is a visual example of the format with the assumption the presentation contains eight key sections.

We have yet to discuss style of delivery. Delivery is key to increasing your power, confidence, and presence.

One suggestion regarding delivery that can have great impact is called the Immersion Technique of the 1/3rd . . . 2/3rds Format. It is

VISUAL EXAMPLE
THE ⅓RD . . . ⅔RDS CONDENSED PRESENTATION FORMAT

POINT 1	POINT 2	POINT 3	POINT 4	POINT 5	POINT 6	POINT 7	POINT 8
INTRO/ THANK YOU	COMPANY BACK-GROUND	CORE OFFERINGS BACK-GROUND	NET BENEFITS	CLIENTS SERVED	CLIENT SUCCESSES	HOW CAN WE HELP YOU?	NEXT STEPS
⅓RD OF THE CONTENT PRESENTED	⅓RD OF THE CONTENT PRESENTED	⅓RD OF THE CONTENT PRESENTED	⅓RD OF THE CONTENT PRESENTED	⅓RD OF THE CONTENT PRESENTED	⅓RD OF THE CONTENT PRESENTED	⅓RD OF THE CONTENT PRESENTED	⅓RD OF THE CONTENT PRESENTED
⅔RDS OF THE CONTENT READY TO BE COVERED ON THIS POINT — IF THE RECIPIENTS ASK YOU TO GO DEEPER ON THIS POINT	⅔RDS OF THE CONTENT READY TO BE COVERED ON THIS POINT — IF THE RECIPIENTS ASK YOU TO GO DEEPER ON THIS POINT	⅔RDS OF THE CONTENT READY TO BE COVERED ON THIS POINT — IF THE RECIPIENTS ASK YOU TO GO DEEPER ON THIS POINT	⅔RDS OF THE CONTENT READY TO BE COVERED ON THIS POINT — IF THE RECIPIENTS ASK YOU TO GO DEEPER ON THIS POINT	⅔RDS OF THE CONTENT READY TO BE COVERED ON THIS POINT — IF THE RECIPIENTS ASK YOU TO GO DEEPER ON THIS POINT	⅔RDS OF THE CONTENT READY TO BE COVERED ON THIS POINT — IF THE RECIPIENTS ASK YOU TO GO DEEPER ON THIS POINT	⅔RDS OF THE CONTENT READY TO BE COVERED ON THIS POINT — IF THE RECIPIENTS ASK YOU TO GO DEEPER ON THIS POINT	⅔RDS OF THE CONTENT READY TO BE COVERED ON THIS POINT — IF THE RECIPIENTS ASK YOU TO GO DEEPER ON THIS POINT

TIME ALLOTTED FOR PRESENTATION—30 MINUTES

not considered high-tech, even though it can be structured that way. (It was for my main platform keynote addresses at Microsoft's World Fusion Annual Conventions with several thousand people in attendance.)

The net-net of the Immersion Technique is this: When recipients enter the room where the presentation will be given, what they should see on the walls are flip charts hanging around the room that have been folded up to the top, so attendees can't see what is on each chart. The flip charts should be hanging on the walls around the room in horseshoe fashion. As people take their seats and the presentation begins, the presenter stands up and begins by unveiling each flip chart—one by one. As they move through the content, the presenter moves around the room, which is why this is called the Immersion Technique. The presenter is on their feet and much more energized as the content is presented. The movement required by the participants (so they can see each chart) is also part of the planned magic. The attendees have to move their bodies a bit as each chart is being unveiled. By the end of the first third of the presentation, all flip charts should be down and presented. Once this happens, recipients can see *the entire presentation* before them much more easily than on PowerPoint. This allows them to remember what's been covered. The questions come faster, and the tone is livelier. Some of our clients say it's more exciting to be a part of this type of presentation. We provide training on this technique if you are serious about having your people become more dynamic presenters.

Without a doubt, this Accelerant principle has many layers and applications. As you might imagine, there are numerous versions of the 1/3rd . . . 2/3rds Condensed Presentation Format, depending on the various stages of the selling and courting process. You will have different iterations for prospect and new business presentations, final presentations to win an opportunity, concept-oriented presentations around big ideas, opportunities recently lost, etc.

Many Accelerants are content rich—easily filling several three-ring binders. This is another of the Accelerants that can be amplified with training and application customization to reformat your company's standard boilerplate presentations—so you begin to DELIVER THE ULTIMATE PRESENTATION.

PAINT THE FINANCIAL PICTURE

*T*HIS ACCELERANT IS ABOUT USING THE FINANCIALLY METRICED VALUE propositions you've created in the fourth principle, which you've packaged into your 1/3rd . . . 2/3rds Condensed Presentation to paint the financial picture of what your new value propositions could deliver, setting a baseline for clients and prospects in your meetings and calls.

Why can it take longer than you'd like for an opportunity to close? One key reason is the presenting company creates *no* sense of urgency to buy. They do a nice job of describing who they are as an organization, the clients they serve, and an overview of their products and services. However, they stop short of tying it all together in a cohesive package. Instead, they expect the prospective buyer to do that by building the business case and financial cost justification for the purchase on their own. There is a better way to sell in these times of global competition.

If your industry is typical, prospective buyers don't begin building the business case for upper management until they've reviewed all vendor options first, benchmarking a few, and narrowing their

selection to a handful of finalists. Only then will they turn their attention to creating the business case and financial picture for their internal presentation to the "higher-ups." (Remember, it's the metrics they seek if all other features and benefits look vanilla to them.) Maybe it doesn't work exactly this way in your business, but it is a common purchasing pattern in many industry sectors.

Could you shorten your closing cycle(s) if you changed a few of your company's standard operating procedures? This is another aspect of the selling cycle that would benefit from such a move. Typically, it's the business case containing the financial picture that is not only necessary for a decision, but the glue that ties everything together, creating the interest and urgency to move forward. Many companies blow it at this juncture, electing to present their "same-old-same-old" without providing any financial picture as to "Why us and why our solution/product/service?" This is a tragedy because it creates work for the buyer. But you've already done the work for this Accelerant.

Using previous Accelerant principles, you've created a more compelling value proposition containing one or two metrics in some form. You should have one or two decision makers in front of you more frequently, because you've successfully ACCESSED THE CASTLE and are armed with a tighter, more powerful presentation that will knock their socks off. The question now becomes, What are you going to present?

The answer should be the frosting—the icing on the cake—the financial picture or metrics that answer the question "Why us?" You referred to this in your letter. Therefore, this is exactly what you should open with at the beginning of your new 1/3rd . . . 2/3rds presentation because this is what sets the hook and begins to generate urgency in the prospective buyer's mind.

Here is an example. As I've mentioned, earlier in my career I sold predictive-dialing networks to large and midsized organizations throughout North America and Europe. Part of the financial picture we painted was that we could more than likely double the talk time of each collector in their department. This was the hook in the first meeting. All we wanted prospects to do was ask, "How?" In fact, truth be told, they really didn't care how the technology worked, especially the senior executives, but they did want to know how we could double their collectors' talk time. Some would bark, *"If you can do this, I'm listening. What do you need to know from us? What data do you need from our people so you can come back here and show us how you can do that?"* *Perfect.* The hook was set. In fact, this was exactly what we used as part of our strategy to quicken the close at Fingerhut, Citigroup, Harris Bank, HFC, I.C. System, and several other companies.

As we've already discussed, you and your team will have to decipher what your metrics will be within the financial picture you wish to paint—an important exercise for your company. Add this frosting to your value proposition, painting the financial picture as to "Why us and our firm." This will set the hook and create more urgency than usual, because often there is none. When the prospective buyer asks how you can verify your frosting statements, you have a *golden* opportunity to collapse your closing cycle by selling them on the need to do a minibusiness case.

You should propose a condensed financial analysis at the front end of their shopping process instead of the "normal" way this is done, toward the end of their search and selection process. To do this, you should create a Value Proposition Validation Instrument— a snapshot of the before-and-after scenarios with your product, service, or solution. We can help you build this.

When you set the hook with your frosting statement and the financial picture you paint feels compelling to them, they will naturally want to know how you can prove it. So the questions in your Value Proposition Validation Instrument will need to extract the key information and data points you need that will enable you to come back and present the financial validation of your value proposition.

Another benefit of proposing some form of minicondensed financial "before and after" overview earlier in the sales cycle is that it helps smoke out prospective buyers' level of interest.

Clients who use this approach love the fact that by getting out onto the table early on in their presentation, the financial net-net of how they can benefit the prospect or client helps them gauge whether the opportunity is worth further time, attention, and resources. They feel it's like a laser beam that helps cut right to the chase. This is a refreshingly open, direct, and honest way to present your offerings in a manner that the sophisticated buyer actually respects and appreciates.

Once they've seen the financial snapshot, it helps you either further galvanize their interest or weed out those who are just browsing.

This approach also assists you in staying connected to the top of the organization because, at the end of the day (as senior executives love to say), it's the financial, quantitative, or metric picture that usually creates the urgency and cost justification to move forward.

Paint the Financial Picture as much as humanly possible in your quest to shorten the closing cycles of your business and your time to a deal. It's an approach that has yielded good results for many. If you want some help in this area, contact us. You might be surprised at how minimal the investment for the return it can deliver.

HOLD YOUR GROUND

HOLD YOUR GROUND

*H*AVE YOU EVER BEEN FOOLED, BIG TIME, AFTER COMING AWAY FROM a meeting you thought went supremely well? A meeting where the primary decision maker(s) were present, told you they were impressed, and wanted to move forward with the next step of your process? A meeting where you were so excited you couldn't contain yourself, so you quickly called your boss and told him or her, "This one's going to go forward." A meeting where you heard, with your own ears, the decision makers say, "We need to do this. This is outstanding."

The eighth Accelerant principle is about the dance of power and how to handle situations when the executives who are expressing their interest in moving forward with you actually might not have any interest in doing anything and are afraid of telling you so, as odd as this may sound.

Ego is something everyone deals with in business. In some cases, the higher you are in an organization, the more likely you'll interface with someone with ego—perhaps a lot of it. Don't misunderstand me. Ego is a good thing because it provides a person with confidence. But it can also get in the way.

Owners and senior executives like people who have strong egos and demonstrate confidence, flair, and guts. It's almost as if they have an attraction to these traits—maybe it reminds them of themselves.

Now, imagine you and your company appearing on the scene (ACCESSING THE CASTLE) with TEETH in your message. You're feeling powerful because you're about to unleash your 1/3rd . . . 2/3rds Presentation, which has so much frosting in the value propositions, you predict they'll be eating right out of your hand. At this point, you're pretty self-confident with swagger in your step and new-found enthusiasm in your presentation.

Here is where you need to be aware of a little trick prospective buyers play as you approach with your financial pictures. Some prospects will do exactly as you want, agreeing to provide the information you need to create the analysis so you can return and present the mini financial picture of before versus after. Others, however, may say something like this:

"You know what? I am impressed with your message and what you say you can do—most impressed. I had no idea you people and your products could have the type of impact on our business you are saying you could have—and for our clients as well. So here's what I'd like to do next. I'd like you to present this to our person in_____, and if they are as enthused about this message as I am, then this is something we really need to look at, all right?"

Upon hearing this, the tongues of many vendors hang out, panting like dogs' because they interpret the statement as a green light, a buying signal. Not that I'm an old dog, but I have been selling for twenty-plus years and won't tell you the number of times I have fallen for this bone. I will tell you that I have not closed one lick of business when I've fallen for it.

You have already invested time and energy developing metrics in your value propositions, which are tight and compelling. You have also developed a relatively short, painless process that allows you to glean information from prospective buyers so you can return and present the before and after in meeting two. If the people in the initial meeting aren't serious enough to be present in the second meeting to hear the results of the minianalysis, *do not* allow them to send you down into the basement of their organization on a wild goose chase, hoping to garner interest. Do not take this bone. There is no business in the basement. Hold your ground. This is a classic trick that many senior executives will use just to get you out of their office when they don't have the guts to tell you the truth. Instead, they'll get vendors all revved up, saying how impressed they are, then send them to the basement, where someone else will stop their progress.

The reason I'm so empathetic about this is because it's happened to me and my clients more than I care to admit. One of our smaller clients met with the CEO of one of the largest firms on Wall Street who seemed quite impressed with their offerings, and said so. The CEO then walked my client down the hall, over to his head of private client services. This was the guy who basically unwound the opportunity so fast my client didn't even know what was happening.

When you sense this happening, draw them out and negotiate, gaining their commitment to be present in the second meeting. If they won't commit to attend, then don't agree to do the minianalysis. You see, because you have set the hook they want to see this before and after. This is not a hard-core approach; it is smart business that reinforces your belief in your message. If they aren't willing to invest the time to understand what the financial benefits or metrics would be, then it doesn't make sense to invest the time and energy to do the exercise. This is the leverage you negotiate with. Sometimes it works, and other times it doesn't. But the approach is worth every penny.

Remember, buyers can be liars. If prospects are impressed with the frosting on your cake, then hold your ground until they've had a real taste. This demonstrates business acumen, prudence, and confidence—all things a sharp prospective buyer likes and respects. They will understand what you are doing and why and appreciate the level of professionalism. Hold your ground. You will be pleased you did.

Here's another example of how a small client (fewer than ten employees) calling on a huge corporation (more than thirty billion dollars in revenues and one of the largest technology corporations in the world) used this Accelerant to save thousands of dollars in selling expenses.

They implemented the Accelerants and went right to the top with their message and request for a meeting. The top officers actually saw the letters, and several were routed downward, one landing about twelve levels below where the client wanted a meeting.

This gentleman, one of several in the curriculum design group within North American sales and services, wanted to take a meeting with our client. Our client probed a bit and discovered that even though one of the top officers had written on his copy of the letter that the offer sounded interesting and was worth checking into, there would be at least another eight to ten meetings before any decision was made. Our client decided it was not worth the selling cost to pursue, so they walked away. They never took the first meeting because this account would be too expensive and time consuming to land.

Hold your ground. You'll assess and smoke out opportunities faster and redirect your resources toward those that will grow your business faster.

NINTH ACCELERANT PRINCIPLE
CONDUCT THE CONCERT

YOU HAVE DETERMINED THAT THE OPPORTUNITY AT HAND IS WORTH pursuing. The prospect has agreed that you can create a condensed financial analysis to validate the financial claims you've made in your initial meeting. Now it's time to CONDUCT THE CONCERT. This Accelerant is the baton that will help persuade the blockers to "stand down" while you extract the various data points and information you need from the various departments within the prospect organization, to validate your value proposition(s).

Remember the Value Proposition Validation Instrument from the seventh Accelerant? This is a snapshot of the before-and-after scenarios with your product or service, which will help validate the potential financial benefits of your core offerings. Again, these are the specific questions that you have prepared to give the prospective buyer, so that they can collect the answers for you, such that you can then plug into this information, how your offerings would improve the prospect's current situation—allowing them to see the "before-your-offerings-versus-after-your-offerings" scenario.

You need a tool like this because even though the powers that be

have given their okay and are often eagerly waiting for you to return and show them the results of your mini high-level ROI analysis, you will face obstacles when it comes to getting the data from their organization.

Because most companies make decisions in groups or teams (even when you are told there is one primary decision maker), there are often several people who have some level of influence on whether or not you win business. Some call them meddlers. Others call them recommenders, influencers, handlers, turf protectors, blockers, etc. They are the group of people you need to orchestrate and conduct like a maestro on the way to the closing concert.

I cannot overstate how important it is to keep all of these people on the same sheet of music. Over the years, we have noticed that one of the best ways to do this is to keep the financial frosting (the metrics) in your value proposition foremost on their minds. That way, you can effectively conduct the concert of extracting the data points you need from the prospective buyer. Because there are so many different agendas within companies, one of the most effective ways to help prospective buyers stay focused on your message is to constantly remind them of the business value—the financial value your offerings could deliver to their enterprise.

No two validation instruments look the same because they are a function of the questions you will need to ask, and their answers will help you make your case. Without this tool, it is easier for the handlers and meddlers lurking behind every other door to slow down or block you from getting the information you need to justify their making an expenditure on your products and services.

Make sure that somewhere toward the top of your printed Value Proposition Validation Instrument you remind anyone who might see the document of the financial claims you've made in your initial value propositions. You must also state that the purpose of this exercise is to get the specific information that will validate just how close you could actually come to the initial teeth in your value proposition(s).

In our first company, I used this tool all the time not only to justify our worth to senior management, but also to stay away from the IT organization—at least until we had a general agreement that the financial outcomes we could deliver were exciting enough to the senior executives that we knew we had a legitimate chance of winning the business. The Value Proposition Validation Instrument acted as an effective leveler with various people who attempted to insert themselves into the process. It prevented them from making it harder than it needed to be for us to get the necessary data from finance, credit and collections, operations, and IT.

We have assisted clients in building these instruments from a content and design standpoint, so they appear basic and easy to follow for the senior officers you'll go back to.

This one-note song of focus reminds them why you need the information because they will ask. And to muddle the music even more at any time in the courting process, various people will attempt to sidetrack you or your offerings. This is nothing new. There are certain folks who just plain don't care or are lazy turf protectors. And there's never a shortage of people who will say, "There's no budget for that," or "We don't need what you offer because we already have something similar." This tool enables you to conduct the concert of gaining the information you need from prospective clients so you can return and justify your value, helping you close, or in the words of Accelerant number ten, harmonize for gold.

HARMONIZE FOR GOLD

*T*HIS ACCELERANT IS SHORT AND SWEET, AND YOU'VE ALREADY DONE most of it if you've metriced your message in Accelerant four.

One of the goals of this process is to be efficient by reusing the work of certain Accelerants to increase the power and effectiveness of the entire tool set. This way, the process is seamless and easy to use. This is what you are doing when you HARMONIZE FOR GOLD.

Assuming you have METRICED YOUR MESSAGE, your value proposition is more articulate regarding the financial outcomes/ deliverables your products, services, or solutions could drive for the prospect or client. This means you're probably more enthusiastic about your message and more excited about getting out there to present it—another outcome of metrics in your value proposition. So there's no need to recreate the wheel. Let's use what you've already done. You can do this by carrying the same financial message you've already created and presented all the way through your meetings, right up to the close and Harmonize for Gold. Simply stated, you are harmonizing for gold when you remind the prospective

HARMONIZE FOR GOLD

buyer (in each meeting or call) of the financial net-net of how your offerings could impact their business.

This involves no tricks or gimmicks. Just a common, financially calibrated value proposition that your prospect saw in your first letter or e-mail to them, all the way through your meetings, conference calls, Web conferences, e-mails, beta tests, etc. Now, you close them with the same or similar message (once your validation instrument helps tweak your original value proposition). See this principle in action in the success story on page 175.

It is comforting to prospective buyers when your message remains consistent throughout the entire process. This builds trust and confidence, helping you close faster.

By and large, the individuals you want to do business with—or more business with—want more safety and security in the decisions they make, because the environment around them continues to be less and less secure. Missteps can cost careers. People are not only aware of that, but become increasingly nervous as they draw closer to any important decision they are involved in making.

Therefore, vendors and providers who can roll up their sleeves and get into the mud, helping prospects build the financial picture and minibusiness case, often win the business. These same providers are also difficult to supplant or replace once they've secured the business, because of a feeling of comfort and safety that's been established between the client and provider. The client feels the provider gets it. In other words, they understand how to help link and package the data they have gleaned for the value proposition validation into a cohesive financial picture. They have clearly connected the *teeth*—the quantifiable benefits of their product or service—to the goals and objectives of the company, so a decision can be made in less time and with more comfort and security.

This is the provider who understands how to Harmonize for Gold and will continue to be a formidable competitor. They have implemented the previous Accelerants, from ASSESSING THEIR STATUS TO CONDUCTING THE CONCERT, to close larger opportunities in a reduced time horizon, to the dismay of their direct competitors.

ELEVENTH ACCELERANT PRINCIPLE
CALIBRATE FOR SUCCESS

*H*AVE YOU EVER SHOT A PERFECT ROUND OF GOLF? DO THE PROFES-sionals typically shoot perfect rounds all the time? If you're a tennis player, is it normal for you to serve aces in every game? Is it normal to perform any sport at peak levels all of the time? Of course not, and the same goes for your business.

As you integrate the Accelerants into your daily culture for hunting and gathering more business, be realistic. Know there will be some false starts and speed bumps along the way. These principles are field proven and require thought if you want to integrate and implement them around your specific goals and objectives.

That is why the Accelerant Process is so beautiful. You can use specific principles to further bolster areas where you need immediate help, or operationalize the entire process for each group of prospects, clients, and in-progress opportunities you wish to target.

Managing your level of expectations is therefore important as you and your organization become comfortable using them in your business. Like everything else in life, sometimes things don't work exactly the way you thought they were going to right out of the gate.

CALIBRATE FOR SUCCESS

It is important to grant yourself both time and patience, making the commitment to work with the tools, shaping them around how they can best serve your needs as a businessperson and as an organization.

To be prudent, we recommend that clients do a pilot—an Accelerant initiative in one or two business units to begin the process. This accomplishes three things: It helps you test the waters with this new process, allows you to benchmark and monitor the results, and helps you gauge how the people involved will respond. The initiative will also create some friendly internal competition and excitement about "who gets to be next" to use the tools.

Clients who calibrate the Accelerant Process to fit their needs have found it a useful, manageable, and rewarding way to allow them time to tweak the way they've run certain training sessions and executive workshops around key Accelerants. This helps them further tailor the initiative around each business unit's unique offerings, characteristics, and market challenges. A unit-by-unit approach keeps everything more manageable and helps the organization track where the greatest successes are coming from, so they can replicate those successes across the organization. Furthermore, if you believe in rewarding and recognizing your people for achieving certain benchmarks, why not build those reward benchmarks into each Accelerants initiative throughout the organization, essentially creating a little old-fashioned, healthy internal competition? You'll further cement the principles into your operating culture, signaling senior management's support and expectations of these tools in all business units. This will result in one common language for targeting, hunting, and closing more business in a compressed time horizon.

It is common for clients—once they have implemented Accelerants on real opportunities—to make adjustments. They may tweak the metrics in their message, adjust the audiences they are targeting to Access the Castle, and continue to refine their 1/3rd . . . 2/3rds Condensed Presentation as they become more proficient in their delivery. For example, some clients initially use the Circle of Leverage tool set to gain access at the very top, and then learn, once they're in, that maybe they went too high. So they will select different targets as they get used to how the methodology works.

Several years back, a major player in the payroll services industry hired me to speak at their annual sales and management kickoff. With about seven hundred people in attendance, the client wanted a keynote focused around the high points of Accelerant five, Access the Castle. Upon concluding the keynote and receiving a standing ovation, I was touched with this groups' genuine drive to get out there and do it. The management was pleased with their employees' aggressive attitude and desire to try it out. I spoke with the management afterward, cautioning them that the COL System is a powerful tool, and that they might want to spend some time thinking through who would be using it, where, on which targets, and on which clients and prospects. The response I got was basically, "Yeah, yeah, yeah. Good point. We'll consider that. Thanks for the heads-up."

Within about sixty to ninety days, I heard that a large part of the sales organization had been turned loose, using the COL tool set in the field. They loved it. But management had not put in place any coordinated rules among the regions as to which companies, titles, etc., should be targeted. So several hundred salespeople were unleashed nationwide with a tool that could bring them more commission because it could help them get to the right people faster. But this was done without much thought from management around implementing a coordinated, strategic approach in using the COL tool wisely to grow their top line with key accounts, prospects, key vertical sectors, and deals already in progress. As a result, I heard some of the same companies were "targeted" simultaneously by salespeople in different regions of the same company, asking for an appointment to pitch their services. How would your company respond if it was approached within the same month or two by two or three divisions of the same company, asking for an appointment?

I am not trying to steer you away from using the tool. My point is that you need to think through the various tools and calibrate them for success. Once your people have been trained on the core Accelerants, have a plan as to how and where you want them used so you experience maximum impact. You don't get into a race car until you've had coaching on how to drive it and full coordination of your team. The same is true for using these tools, regardless of the size of your sales and marketing force. They are advanced tools and require some thought around how and where they should be implemented to accomplish your desired outcomes.

Our clients also make modifications to their Value Proposition Validation Instrument after they've used it a few times. They'll add certain questions they forgot to include, change the format of the document, etc. This is what I mean when I say Calibrate for Success. As clients incorporate these principles into their business, it is normal to experience growing pains that need attention. This helps hone the principles so they serve the highest and best use of the organization.

Selling is a process because the market is constantly in motion. Calibrating for Success helps you continually tweak and fine-tune the Accelerants around the different types of businesses you target for the products, services, and solutions you bring to the marketplace, giving your company maximum benefit.

COMPLETE THE CIRCLE
OF INTEGRATION

COMPLETE THE CIRCLE
OF INTEGRATION

*W*HEN YOU EXPERIENCE SUCCESS IN ONE PART OF YOUR BUSINESS, don't you look to replicate that success in other areas? This is something we suggest with Accelerants because of their applicability and value to multiple areas within your business.

This is what this Accelerant is all about, completing the process so you've got one common sales methodology for targeting, hunting, and closing more business throughout your enterprise. It's about creating a common language flexible enough to be tailored to the unique challenges of each business unit, so that as you experience success in your first Accelerant initiative, you can complete the integration by continuing its application in other business units to amplify its effectiveness throughout your enterprise.

One of the aspects business leaders like about this process is that it's circular and ongoing. Business professionals like processes with a distinct beginning and end point—circular in design, stressing continual improvement. CEOs can stand in front of their organizations at sales meetings or before analysts on Wall Street and share the Accelerant Process, explaining how they analyzed each constraint's effect on their business. They can then walk these audiences through each Accelerant tool, explaining its value to their organization, how it will minimize the constraints over time, how it will make the organization's people more effective, and how the organization can tailor the process to each business unit's unique challenges to increase top-line revenues while reducing the cost of sales.

The Accelerant Process is a logical process that senior management, your field force, analysts, shareholders, and bankers can understand. It will give them confidence that you *have* a proven process that everyone can follow to help drive your growth for the next ten years and beyond.

As you know, most successful businesspeople don't jump in with both feet when it comes to a new concept or process. They want to be prudent, testing the procedure on particular opportunities or in specific business units that need help right away or pose the least risk if things don't go quite right. But once they experience success, they like to replicate it in other business units and with opportunities where they desire the same boost.

Embedding these principles into the DNA of your company's strategic targeting, hunting, and business-gathering process can have a measurable impact on growing your top line, compressing your time to a deal, reducing the cost of securing business, and enhancing the margins on the business gained. The case histories in Section Three evidence this success.

Because you have now done the work, why not extend the value of your investment by bringing key aspects like your new value propositions into other areas that impact revenue growth? For example, clients who integrate certain Accelerants like Metric the Message into their marketing communications, collateral, and executive white papers show prospects and clients one cohesive message throughout all their materials.

The same is true if you applied Accelerants to your customer service and contact call centers. Why not have each customer-facing account representative know how to articulate your new financially metriced value propositions? Equip them with the ability to explain how you can deliver upon that message. You'd be surprised how your people will become better at upselling your customer base, driving even more incremental revenue. This is a continued push to show prospects and clients one united, cohesive face and message. Accelerants can also help boost results at trade shows, conventions, and user meetings. Consider using them in your public relations, advertising, direct mail, and Internet-based promotions. This way, you will Complete the Circle of Integration by maximizing the value these principles can generate for your organization.

As mentioned, the Accelerant Process for Business operationalizes these principles on existing clients, prospects, vertical industry opportunities, and in-progress situations you have determined are worthy of focus and resources. What this means is, once clients have done the work suggested around each of the tools, they then implement their new process on opportunities they feel are worthy of hunting, to bring in more business.

Clients initially move through each principle at a more relaxed pace if this is their first time. The intensity and calibration of the Accelerants depends on the volume of targeted companies in a given time frame. Clients interested in systematizing their approach to key vertical industry sectors, stepping things up a notch or two, often move to Accelerant Campaigns. These are more aggressive scenarios in which you approach several directly competing companies simultaneously, presenting a common value proposition, with the goal of quickening the overall response rate.

This has proven a precise strike-force approach to systematically hunting and gathering more business in a particular region or vertical. It has also delivered results in national campaigns. Read about the results of this approach in the upcoming success stories. Accelerants are effective tool sets, and an effective business improvement process, whether targeting one, two, or several companies in a given time frame.

Numerous clients, from small privately held companies to mid-sized and multinational enterprises, have experienced success by implementing these tools. Some have given themselves a growth spurt. Others have employed specific principles, making them a part of their standardized business development processes.

To provide a flavor of testimonials lending credence to the principles' validity and usefulness, three additional Success Stories follow, showcasing the principles in different scenarios and giving you an idea of the diversity in which they can operate and provide value.

"Climbing the Mountain" is about one of the companies I founded—a small, privately held vendor attempting to sell its predictive-dialing technology to a billion-dollar, direct-mail catalog marketer (Fingerhut Corporation) and going head to head with a few large technology companies such as the old IBM-Rolm, AT&T, Rockwell, and others.

"Run-Build-Run" deals with a multinational management consulting, systems integration, and outsourcing firm that used an aggressive Accelerant Campaign on a defined number of companies. Their goal was to sell and close large-volume, multiyear contracts for a particular service offering designed to jump-start their revenue line and increase their global competitiveness in this specific area.

"Selling Executive Aircraft" deals with a small, privately held start-up publishing a high-end executive aircraft publication. One Accelerant Campaign Blitz put their publication on the map—creating strong cash flow and demand for their services. There was no need to raise capital to get off the ground—their publication was already in flight.

Each story is real. To honor client confidentiality, some company names cannot be revealed. But you will hear enough specifics to paint a clear picture of what happened and the results that followed.

Section Three

THREE MORE ACCELERANT SUCCESS STORIES

ACCELERANT SUCCESS STORY: CLIMBING THE MOUNTAIN

In our small start-up, with less than two years under our belt and closing cycles around six to eighteen months, cash flow was tight. It was the blind leading the blind, finding our way as new entrepreneurs selling high-end technology, which we had never done before. Our products, called call-progress machines, were becoming known as predictive-dialing systems. We were at the beginning of new technology and had to explain what the machines did and the value they could provide on every appointment.

Because we were small, it was easy to Assess Our Status. We didn't have much going on, period! If we wanted to make any money, we'd need to start chasing some big fish. We knew what we wanted our future to look like, so we began doing research on companies in our backyard—large credit and collection operations. To my surprise, one of the larger public companies in Minneapolis had a remote collections operation staffed with several hundred collectors, running two shifts per day, six days a week. We had no contacts at this firm—none—and none of my relationships knew any key executives, so accessing this mountain of an organization was going to be a challenge. We would have to hit them aggressively, with a bold, metriced message, just to get their attention.

Upon further digging, I learned they were an IBM client, running two large mainframes that, among other things, kept track of one-million-plus customers throughout the country.

After determining this was a company worth targeting, common sense told us we had two choices: One was to Access the Castle at the director of collections level and try to create enough urgency and enthusiasm for our message and technology, hoping they had enough juice to take us to the correct powers that be. The other was to approach where everyone else seemed to go in, which was inside the IT organization.

Since this company's IT organization was substantial (several hundred people) and because going the IT route immediately put us at risk of being relegated to a long list entitled "another IT project for review someday," I decided to step back and think through how we could collapse our selling time by entering higher in the organization with a tighter message that was basically all about the numbers—the financials—and not about the technology.

If we could get to the right audience, and they were impressed enough with the financial story, maybe those executives could drive the opportunity from the top down, creating enough urgency within the IT organization to review our solution much faster and benchmark and bless the technology so we could close the business in less time.

We had Chartered Our Course and were locked on this mountain, convincing ourselves we had nothing to lose. To Metric the Message now became our focus. How could we take a bunch of really cool technology (hardware, software, and services) and shift the prospects attention totally off the technology and onto the financial results it delivered? This became our messaging strategy—especially since several competitors, such as IBM-Rolm, AT&T, and Rockwell, were all talking about their technology and its marvelous features and benefits.

We knew from experience that many top executives—with the exception of the CIO—really didn't care much about how the technology worked, just that it did. They were more interested in what it could deliver in financial terms. Therefore, we set about grinding down our value proposition—putting as much teeth into it as possible, hoping that when we approached, it would act as a heat-seeking laser, bringing us to the senior people who could drive change, cut through bureaucracy, and cause things to happen.

We agreed that talking about our technology in the initial meetings would slow us down and potentially dust us all together, since our multibillion-dollar competitors wielded bigger budgets and hundreds of technology client references versus our one client. Did I mention we were small?

By grinding down our message, it became clear that one of the primary benefits of predictive-dialing technology was its ability to increase the talk time of each collector. We knew most manual collection floors without this technology were actually talking with debtors an average of eighteen to twenty-four minutes per hour hour, per collector. The remaining time was burned figuring out who to call next, dialing the number, listening to rings, busy signals, three-tones, etc. Our prospect was a manual operation. Our automated systems could get their talk time up to forty-two to forty-five minutes per hour and basically double the talk time for each collector. Since they employed several hundred collectors per shift, two shifts daily, six days a week, the simple mathematics of our financial picture would be compelling. This is the frosting statement we led with in our COL approach letter. Here is the gist of what we wrote in our value proposition:

"We have the ability to nearly double the individual talk time of each one of your collectors, from what we believe it is now—eighteen to twenty-four minutes per hour—to around forty-two to forty-five minutes out of every hour.

"This essentially gives your organization one of two choices. Either you can employ the same number of collectors and perhaps double your collections monthly, or, you could maintain the same level of debtors you are currently reaching—but with half as many collectors. This means you could reduce your payroll and insurance benefits on these individuals by millions of dollars. The choice would obviously be yours.

"This is our value proposition to your organization. If you allow us an appointment at the right executive level, we offer a free mini ROI business analysis, which would serve to validate our numbers and claims—so you have an even clearer picture of what the real financials would look like for your organization. I hope you will accept our offer, allowing us to substantiate how we could double the productivity levels of your collections operation through our free mini ROI business analysis."

Now that we had Metriced the Message, our confidence level went up a notch or two. We were jazzed about taking it to them, so it was time to nail down where we should enter within the castle. By doing the work on the message, it became evident that approaching the IT organization was probably not wise, since they'd force us back onto a conversation about our technology, which we didn't want because it would drag out a potential sale by months. Approaching the director of collections didn't feel right either— probably too low in the organization. What if that individual had built the collections operation and was happy with its size? Then we'd be toast.

By using the COL approach from Accelerant principle five, Access the Castle, we targeted several senior officers who we thought might care about our message, if they saw it. We researched the names and titles of the individuals over each major division and function of the company and selected the president/CEO, CFO, SVP of finance, SVP of credit and collections, and SVP of operations.

We broadcast our value proposition via the COL letter to these five executives, asking for assistance and guidance on getting a meeting with the most appropriate senior people. We explained that we wanted to present our story and gain their agreement on doing the mini ROI business analysis (our value proposition instrument). Not knowing where we would land inside the castle, I fired off custom letters to each of the five executives, regular mail.

Almost like waving a magic wand, we were in. Two top financial people were asking, "How? How can you do this? What do you need to know from us to validate these numbers and do your analysis?" It was outstanding. And because I had asked for a fifteen-minute appointment, making sure it was painless for them to grant—my 1/3 presentation was done in about five minutes. The sole purpose in being there was to gain their agreement to provide us the data from their collections operation so we could do our analysis and return to present the findings. That was it. They agreed, so we didn't need to Hold Our Ground this time.

It appeared the IT organization didn't know about the meeting, but we braced for a call from the director of collections. We predicted he would either be defensive once he found out about the meeting or try to shut us down completely out of jealously or spite, because we hadn't approached him first. The call never came. Instead, within a few weeks, we received a fax with the answers to most of our questions regarding their collections operation— enough so we could do the analysis.

Our initial hunches regarding their manual operations were close. We had underestimated the number of collectors, however, so the size of the productivity lift—or labor savings—was more sub-stantial than we had suggested. This would allow us to show them how our technology could pay for itself within eight to nine months. After that, it would deliver pure savings or an increase in dollars collected—the choice was theirs.

Painting the Financial Picture in our COL approach letter had so far helped us avoid conversations about our technology and seemed to keep the two financial executives patient until we pre-sented the ROI analysis. In meeting number two, the same two fi-nancial individuals were present. In less than twenty-five minutes, we had walked them through an Immersion Presentation of the 1/3rd ... 2/3rds Format outlining how we had performed their mini ROI business analysis and the corresponding conclusions of how our systems could deliver the financial story. No PowerPoint, no darkened room. We were up and moving about, keeping the en-ergy and interest levels high. This allowed us to validate our initial value proposition in the letter—using the data they supplied to walk them through how their numbers could be improved with our systems.

They received the information almost in disbelief, with an atti-tude of *"How could this be possible? I mean, your numbers are very compelling. I just thought our collections operation was state of the art—running well above comparable operations around the country."*

The two financial executives called a sixty-minute third meeting and guess who else was present in addition to our two sponsors? If you guessed the CIO, you'd be correct. Also present were the SVP of credit and collections, the vice president of credit and collections, and the director of collection floor operations. I'm not sure I've re-membered the exact number of people and their titles accurately, but you get the picture. We were instructed to re-present our mini ROI business analysis, which we did for twenty minutes, using flip charts and the Immersion Technique of the 1/3rd . . . 2/3rds Format. The tone in the room was friendly and cordial.

Upon finishing the presentation, questions started to fly. You can guess what the CIO asked, based on the fact he had never heard of us or of predictive-dialing technology. His questions were all about the technology. The director of collection floor operations also posed numerous questions and appeared to be the person tasked to provide the collection floor data in order for us to complete the mini ROI business analysis.

The dynamic in the room was fascinating. It was clear the financial picture we painted for the two senior executives had gotten their attention—so much so that within a few weeks, the organization formed a formal task force of approximately ten people and charged them with creating the collection floor and technology requirements specifications for a potential predictive-dialing technology acquisition. An RFI (request for information) was then sent to more than twenty different potential vendors.

We were off to the races. The next twelve months were a long process of monthly, sometimes bimonthly meetings with the task force as they gradually pared their list of potential vendors to a few finalists. During this time the task force christened us "the Flip-Chart Boys." They'd kid us about how we'd unveil our flip charts as we walked around the conference room. (Isn't there an expression that goes, "If they're teasing you that means they like you?") It is my guess we were easier to comprehend than some of our competitors who came in with fancy PowerPoint slideshows and other show-and-tell techniques.

During the year of task force meetings, we used the ninth Accelerant, Conduct the Concert, frequently. It can be easy for any billion-dollar organization to get caught up in their power and size. The financial picture we kept in front of them served as an effective leveler with those attempting to block or slow down our efforts. And my hunch is we probably had higher levels of access to the senior executives than perhaps any of our competitors, based on where we had elected to enter about twelve months earlier.

In the final presentation, after months of detailed meetings, the first third of the presentation took about thirty minutes. What we presented was basically the same financial picture we had shared about twelve months earlier—coupled with a brief, condensed synopsis of why our technology, versus other finalists, was a better answer to their stated technical needs and requirements. A week or two later, we received the call from the head of the task force that we had been selected as their vendor of choice and to return to the company's offices to go over specific terms they wanted in the agreement regarding performance specifications, payment terms, etc.

I couldn't help but wonder how two guys in an upstart just beat out IBM-Rolm, AT&T, Rockwell, and several other formidable competitors. Was it because we had better technology? Or was it because of things a bit harder to define that we did along the way? Things like including metrics in our message, making it much easier to understand why they should talk to us in the first place and investigate this technology a bit deeper. Also, how we Accessed the Castle, which helped us get senior-level traction around our financial message, creating the urgency that caused the task force to be created. Remember, they weren't looking for a solution for their collections operations. So you could say that with these tools, we created an opportunity out of nowhere. We specifically Painted the Financial Picture of the results they could expect to see within certain ranges, and kept Conducting the Concert by reminding them of this. (This consistent financial focus helped mitigate some of the petty politics that popped up along the way with those people who appear in every company, who can't seem to get out of their own way.)

By being concise and easy to follow in all 1/3rd . . . 2/3rds Presentations, did they come to enjoy our visits more than anyone else's? Talk about Delivering the Ultimate Presentation! Even though we were frequently kidded about the old-fashioned nature of the 1/3rd . . . 2/3rds Format, they appreciated its simplicity and brevity— not to mention it was easier to follow. The teasing didn't bother us.

Without question, the Accelerant Principles were invaluable in landing this mountain of an opportunity, which helped put us on the map. It gave us the confidence, momentum, and a repeatable platform we could follow for new opportunities on our Chartered Course.

ACCELERANT SUCCESS STORY: RUN—BUILD—RUN

It is time to share a success from a larger client—a multinational management consulting, technology integration, and outsourcing firm with several practice areas and thousands of talented professionals employed worldwide.

Perhaps your first question would be: Why would a successful global firm with many satisfied clients use Accelerants? I cannot share all details about the specific firms they targeted or the incremental lift in revenues, out of respect for client confidentiality. Suffice it to say they were pleased enough with a five-fold-plus return on their investment that, as best we are aware, the people trained on the tools continue to use them to close larger deals in less time— and to help assess the potential scope of opportunities earlier on in the courting process.

When the dot-com bust cast its spell on the technology industry, spending dramatically contracted over a period of years. The

September 11 terrorist attacks on America followed. Hundreds of technology players of all sizes began to experience fits and starts of every form and fashion. Constant change was the order of the day. This included bankruptcy, Chapters Seven and Eleven, massive downsizing, quarterly reorganizations, office closings, etc.

It was during this time that our firm was retained to assist a large global consultancy in one area, which we'll call Consumer Products–Retail Distribution. The client had created a new service offering they wanted to market aggressively to a targeted group of multibillion-dollar companies nationwide, which they had identified as potential prospects—all in a particular vertical industry. The end game was to close multimillion-dollar, multiyear agreements around this offering we will call Run-Build-Run.

The firm's thinking appeared sound, and they wanted our assistance in reviewing the business strategy, value proposition, and access plan for the senior executives they were targeting to attend the initial capabilities meetings at the firms they had identified.

Because the offering was technology oriented, the client thought meetings with the top technology officer of the target entities—each between two and ten billion in annual revenue—was the appropriate place to start.

After listening to the business objectives, approach strategy, and value proposition of the offering, it appeared there were potential gaps and unresolved questions regarding how the plan would actually come together. My work with the Accelerant Principles had helped us become fairly accurate at spotting potential approach-and-implementation problems before they happened.

We went to work by following the Accelerant Process for Business—applying each Accelerant tool set to their stated objectives and time lines. As with any large consultancy, heavily matrixed organizations such as these can sometimes present confusion for their clients, and for those inside the organization as well, in terms of who's targeting who, and why.

In this case, the practice area charged with finding the revenue for this new offering was expecting leads or referrals from other practice areas within the firm, but these were not coming. Therefore, the decision was made that they would act as their own direct sales organization, targeting this initial group of companies, which seemed like good candidates for a multiyear agreement around this particular offering.

In one sense, you could say they had already Assessed Their Status, Designed Their Future, and Chartered Their Course prior to retaining us. However, as we began putting Teeth into their message—because there were no metrics as far as we were concerned—the client became more open about revisiting the audience they actually wanted in their initial meetings. They knew from experience that these types of transactions could take twelve or more months to hunt, qualify, and close, and they wanted to compress the time horizon if at all possible.

We convinced them that if the metrics—the Teeth—were compelling enough, approaching the CIO or top technology officer was the wrong place to enter, and that the CEO, president, and CFO were better candidates to receive their message, because if they liked it, these people could drive the deals from the top down, and potentially close them faster.

They accepted the logic, so we recalibrated their future, and rechartered their course by grouping certain competitive companies together on their targeted list into an Accelerant Campaign—a more sophisticated blitzing technique designed for situations when it might be necessary or appropriate to approach multiple companies simultaneously with a common value proposition that could benefit all—and where faster action is desired.

By walking through the fifth Accelerant, Access the Castle, they selected three executives they really wanted present in their initial one-hour meeting—the CEO and/or president, the COO, and the CFO. This would be a difficult group to bring together at the same time, in the same room, in the middle of July, when it seems as if all senior management in the United States take their vacations.

The client became convinced that if they could address this audience, they could dramatically collapse their time to a deal. We wrote their multipage COL approach letter, which was calibrated to the three executives they desired in the first meeting, Painting the Financial Picture of a cost-reduction play that could potentially deliver millions in savings over the course of the multiyear term.

We expected and prepared our client for pushback from the technology officer once he or she became aware of the letters, since it was a technology-related offering, and we couldn't prevent the letters from bouncing around inside the organization after they landed. The letter was carefully constructed so as not to alienate our client from the technology officer, but instead, to explain why he or she didn't need to be present in the initial meeting because it was 100 percent about the numbers.

In June and July, we orchestrated an Accelerant Campaign Blitz where our client simultaneously approached thirty-six companies nationwide. All 108 customized COL approach letters arrived with military precision (thirty-six companies, three executives per company). As a result, sixteen organizations granted meetings, and in each meeting except one, the CEO/president, COO (if they employed one), and the CFO were all present in the same room. All sixteen initial meetings were executed in about an eight-week time horizon—choreographed like clockwork.

The client was amazed at the speed of access to these senior executives. They were also delighted to be able to enter at the top of the organization from the beginning and in a different division than they were typically used to initially approaching with this type of offering. They felt that this move helped garner traction faster around their message, which now had more TEETH. To top it off, none of the meetings was canceled—something they were used to—and the officers actually showed up as promised. This was almost too good to be true.

As the client Painted the Financial Picture via their 1/3rd . . . 2/3rds Presentation, approximately five companies agreed to the fee-based financial assessment, which then yielded a few pieces of closed business in far less time than the client was expecting.

They did an artful job of Holding Their Ground and Conducting the Concert, running interference between the technology and finance executives to secure the data they needed to Harmonize for Gold and close.

The Accelerant Process and custom-calibrated Campaign Blitz delivered a much higher caliber of initial meetings, laced with multiple senior executives who had the power and authority to make the decision (in a more comfortable and safer group environment) once they understood the financial picture being painted. This became one of the reasons the opportunities closed more rapidly.

Based on experience, it is my opinion that most large firms rely on their sheer size and/or market dominance to get in the door. The Accelerant Process showed this company new thinking. Truth be told, they really didn't have a problem gaining access, or they wouldn't be a multibillion-dollar multinational. However, what they learned was a tool set that could further compress their time to a deal— something every company wants to do. They implemented this structured methodology and execution strategy for systematically approaching several companies on their radar screen with the goal of closing business in a compressed time horizon. And that is what happened in this initiative. How can the Accelerants help you do something similar?

ACCELERANT SUCCESS STORY: SELLING EXECUTIVE AIRCRAFT

In the heart of the south lies a small, privately held publisher of a high-end, executive aircraft publication. The vision for this exclusive magazine was clearly pictured in the mind of its entrepreneurial founder when he contacted us about his concept. He wondered if the Accelerant Process might help get the magazine launched so he wouldn't need to approach the capital markets to fund the start-up phase. He did not want to give up half the equity in the business to get it off the ground.

The founder was candid about the fact the marketplace didn't need another high-end executive aircraft publication to assist established private aircraft dealers in advertising and selling their inventory. He explained that though it was a "clubby" community that would be difficult to break into, he felt he could provide enough differentiation among the current publications to create and sustain a viable business.

It sounded as if he had partially Assessed His Status, explaining the intensity of the competition and the difficulty of breaking into these established dealers, who had long-term relationships with other publications. It also appeared he had Designed His Future because he was aware that, as the new kid on the block, he would need traction at the very top of the dealers he was targeting. Meetings with the directors of advertising or marketing were not going to fly because decisions would take too long and ultimately would travel up to the executive level anyway.

As he shared the list of forty companies he thought were worthy targets because he believed they could afford the fees for a full-year agreement, we began asking questions. We wanted to understand the length of the closing cycle for this type of advertising sale, the complexity of the sale, and whether any firms on his list were in competition with one another. We also wanted to understand his capacity to handle the business if things went well and he closed 25 percent of the forty companies. In effect, we were asking if he could handle the business if it all came at once—or would he need to turn some of it down?

His feedback helped us initially Charter the Course, which we refined when we learned cash flow was tight and that business needed to land within ninety days or he would be forced to make some unpleasant decisions. We understood and asked for permission to revisit his Chartered Course after we assisted in adding Metrics to the Message and determined how he should best go about rapidly Accessing the Castle of these forty independently owned aircraft dealers throughout the country.

Because the existing publications were established and well done, the TEETH in the offer needed to be exceedingly compelling. He needed a one-two punch articulating why the prospect should either expand their budget and spend additional dollars in a new publication or reallocate dollars away from a publication they were already using. This was a gutsy message indeed, especially for an unknown start-up.

The publisher signed off on the value proposition we helped fashion because we knew from experience where we were going to advise him to enter within these forty companies. Clearly, this client needed signed advertising commitments ASAP, so it would be too risky to Access the Castle at the more traditional level, such as the director of advertising or marketing. Action was what he wanted.

Therefore, we advised that he Access the Castle at the very top—the owner, president, and/or CEO. Due to cash flow needs, he did not hesitate to accept our advice.

The publisher also put together a 1/3rd . . . 2/3rds Presentation that could be delivered via conference call to save money on travel expenses, collapsing the time horizon of signing the business. This was also a unique way of flushing out those companies that were serious from those just window-shopping.

The financial picture painted in the value proposition was strong but necessary, based on the business objectives our client had set forth. We are not at liberty to share the value proposition, but it did contain financial incentives for those willing to pay up front and commit to one full year of advertising.

In a nutshell, the Chartered Course we advised was to play all forty companies against one another by only offering twelve slots to the first twelve aircraft dealers to sign up—in essence, freezing out all others from the flagship launch of the unique publication for one entire year.

Each of the twelve had to commit to the terms and sign a twelve-month agreement by a certain date. The twelve dealers that agreed to participate in year one of the publication would have first dibs on signing up for a second year—continuing to freeze out competitors they might not want to be advertising next to in the same publication. As mentioned, there was also a financial incentive for the initial twelve for signing a commitment to advertise by the required date.

We were very involved in writing, rewriting, and calibrating the five-page Circle of Leverage approach letter to the executive audience the client wanted to access quickly. We employed an Accelerant Campaign Blitz in which all COL custom-written approach letters landed simultaneously with the executives of the forty targeted firms.

It worked. People often want what they can't have, and when

something is offered and then essentially taken away, it sometimes creates the urgency necessary to cause action—if the value proposition is of interest. In this case, it was. At the end of the day, pitting forty companies against one another and boldly communicating that only twelve dealers would be allowed in the flagship first year of the exclusive publication created the initial urgency required to cause action around the offering.

The client reported that even before he had begun the phone follow-ups to learn if the executives were interested in a conference call, some of the owners were calling him with the basic message, *"I'm in. Count me in as one of the twelve. FedEx me the contract for my review."* As you can imagine, the publisher was flying high.

Holding Your Ground and Conducting the Concert didn't seem to be an issue in this engagement. The COL approach letter, coupled with the strategies pace, and the level at which we entered the castle with compelling, time-sensitive TEETH in the value proposition, allowed the client to immediately Harmonize for Gold.

With surprising speed, the client closed and signed twelve advertising commitments within approximately two months and had also collected the initial down payments, avoiding the need to seek start-up capital. He was moving down the runway for takeoff.

With cheerleaderlike enthusiasm, the publisher became a convert to the power and systematic manner in which the Accelerant Process worked. During our debriefing he commented that as soon as he had the initial publication under way, he wanted to repeat the process, using a customized Accelerant Campaign on a different segment of the marketplace to expand his advertiser base for the publication. Here was another client convert to the power the Accelerant Process can deliver when the company takes the time to follow the principles in the order in which they are designed to be used. The results are worth achieving.

There have been numerous client successes where just a few Accelerant Principles delivered a pleasing result for the user. The larger and more important question is Where can Accelerants provide the highest and best use for your business? After you and your people have finished this book, this is an excellent question to discuss with your peers so you can come to consensus on where to begin within your company.

Section Four

MOVING FORWARD

CUSTOMIZING THE PROCESS TO YOUR BUSINESS APPLICATIONS

*L*IKE ANY WELL-ACCEPTED GENERIC SOFTWARE PROGRAM, ACCELERANTS cannot typically perform the myriad applications a company might need without some level of customization. Most tools in the marketplace are designed to perform a baseline of tasks but must be customized around the objectives and desired outcomes of the business before delivering maximum value. And so it is with Accelerants.

The primary purpose of this book has been to share the basic nature of the twelve constraints so you can determine which ones are impeding your company's revenue growth and forward progress. Merely describing the constraints provides value because it helps companies shine a spotlight on issues that are blocking progress.

The Accelerants take things one step further by showcasing each principle and the way they can work together to provide a cohesive solution for your business.

Remember the overwhelming international success of Dr. Stephen R. Covey's *The 7 Habits of Highly Effective People,* where he laid out and described the Seven Habits? It was a very compelling book indeed, and the reaction to it was powerful throughout the world with millions of units sold. I recall listening to many very smart executives describe their reactions to the book and to the Seven Habits.

Some executives thought it was a good read, providing valuable information they could immediately apply in their personal and professional lives without needing to invest in the customization of the Seven Habits around their specific objectives. They felt further investment was not necessary because the content was well presented and explained, allowing them to "take it from there," to use their lingo.

There were and still are plenty of other senior executives and business owners so inspired by the content that the book became an informational tool. These people saw the real value of embracing the habits in their personal and professional lives and were willing to invest further to learn how they could be applied and tailored to their applications, goals, and objectives. These are the people who took the Seven Habits to a higher level, gaining additional benefit.

Covey's book created a training and management consulting business that grew to more than ninety million dollars in annual revenues before being acquired by Franklin Quest. This is an indication of the thousands of businesses and people who invested further in understanding how the habits could best be applied for their own situations, receiving additional value well beyond what the book delivered. In fact, Franklin-Covey claims to serve more than four hundred of the Fortune 500 companies. This validates in some manner that great value has been and continues to be delivered around these timeless principles. What this means is, as you read and perhaps reread this book, you may see how an investment in having your people trained on key Accelerants, then shaping the process around your core offerings and target markets, would warrant an excellent payback. For the many who took Covey's principles to task in their own business, many saw substantial payback. And you could see the same type of payback and ROI as you shape these tools around your key objectives, then train and support your people as they learn to implement the tools in the field against the specific targets you set forth as part of your growth objectives.

As the expression goes, "You get what you pay for." Which path will you choose? I have attempted to provide genuine value within this book so that the descriptions of the constraints and the Accelerants will benefit your business going forward. Some will feel inspired by the simple power and efficiencies of the Accelerants and wish to shape them around their specific business needs to gain an even higher return. You have the opportunity to engage an ACE: an Accelerant Client Executive who can listen to your goals and give you guidance on how best to accomplish your desired outcomes. It would be our pleasure to help you compress your sales cycle(s) and move your business to the next level.

TRANSFERRING THE KNOWLEDGE AND SKILL SETS TO YOUR PEOPLE

*A*S AN EXTENSION OF THE CONVERSATION ABOUT CUSTOMIZING THE Accelerants and the Accelerant Process around your businesses specific applications, let's touch on the next step—transferring the knowledge and skill sets to your people. This topic evokes an age-old argument that management consulting, training and skills development firms battle on a daily basis with clients and prospects.

Time out of the field, as business owners and senior executives describe it, seems to be the sticking point in the debate. Many executives feel time out of the field is nonrecoverable lost productivity that will negatively impact the numbers. My question is, Does it really, or is the real issue that some training programs don't directly impact top-line revenue generation, collapse the time it takes to close an opportunity, or shrink the cost of sales? Perhaps this is why the debate has become so sticky for companies considering an investment in their people's skills and abilities.

The Accelerant Principles and Process are designed to help impact top-line growth, collapse the time to a deal, and reduce the cost of securing business. That being said, how could you argue compellingly that taking your people out of the field for a short period of time would create a loss in productivity if, in fact, the opposite is true? Consider this when investing in a program that can teach your team how to use field-proven tools that could leapfrog their skills and abilities in becoming more proficient and productive so they can do more business.

This appears to be where the conversation should be centered as you consider investing in your people to maximize their proficiencies with the principles.

Certain Accelerants have training programs, consulting modules, and workshops associated with them that focus on a particular Accelerant—both how and why they work and how to most effectively apply them. There are advanced levels of programs as well for those who wish to master the principles. Consulting and ongoing coaching are also available to support those who have completed the training and workshops and are ready to shape the tools around specific applications.

Perhaps it comes down to your personal level of conviction regarding how the Accelerants could positively impact your business for years to come. My suggestion is to keep the "time out of the field" argument in proper perspective because, in the final analysis, your decision to bring your people up to speed on the principles so they can be most effective will far outstrip that argument on any given day.

REAL-WORLD APPLICATION, IMPLEMENTATION, AND EXECUTION

*A*DVANCING ONE STEP FURTHER, THE REAL-WORLD APPLICATION, implementation, and execution of the principles are where the rubber meets the road. In this vein, I have provided success stories throughout the book intended to spur your thinking about how the tools can best provide value for your business.

There are no warning signs on this material, such as "Do not operate heavy machinery while implementing the Accelerants" or "It is important to wear a hard hat and protective eyewear when using Accelerants."

However, common sense should suggest that it might be a good idea (if you're not going to go through the training on key Accelerants) that you begin using them on "B"- or "C"-type opportunities initially. Become familiar with the principles by trying them out on opportunities that are not of dire importance to the business. This will provide you the latitude to take risks, make mistakes, and get used to how the Accelerants might best work for you.

Remember, you get what you pay for. Consider investing in the training or, at the very least, some level of consulting on how to shape the tools around your "A" list opportunities. This would apply no matter what the nature of your business and the price points of your products, services, solutions, or concepts. Great value has been delivered in these situations, as described in the success stories.

One last word about managing your expectations as you implement the principles. If you have never hit a golf ball, or if you're an average player on a good day, is it fair to expect that you will shoot par? Probably not—in fact, of course not. As you begin using the principles, do not expect the world in terms of results. It isn't fair to the principles, nor is it fair to you. Rarely do people lock on to a new approach and master it in a flash. Set your expectations accordingly. Allow for mistakes. That is how you learn the tools and can someday become proficient in their use.

Many who have gone before you have applied the principles and found success. So practice them until you see the results for yourself and experience the power and value of the Accelerants.

Thank you for your time. Good luck and enjoy.

Section Five

WHERE TO TURN FOR ASSISTANCE

THE VALUE OF THE CONSTRAINTS ASSESSMENT AND HOW TO GET IT DONE FOR YOUR BUSINESS

*A*S I EXPLAINED IN THE FIRST ACCELERANT, ASSESS YOUR STATUS, the Constraints Assessment helps you understand and see more clearly those constraints impeding your company's growth. This information is important because it will help you not only address them, but also determine the ones that need to be corrected right away.

This process can shed valuable light because the individuals taking the assessment are you, the management team, and the individuals within marketing, sales, business development, customer service, field consultants, and field management whose opinions are valued within the company. This is why the feedback is relevant—it comes from your own people. And once you are able to review the information, you can make better decisions about how to Design Your Future and Charter Your Course.

You have options in terms of the assessment, based on the size of your company and the number of people you'd like to participate. Your choices also include an onsite visit by our team to conduct the assessment or perhaps doing it online. To learn more, please visit www .accelerantinternational.com and click on the Constraints Assessment.

ABOUT ACCELERANT INTERNATIONAL PRODUCT AND SERVICE OFFERINGS—CLIENTS SERVED

WHY MIGHT YOU BE INTERESTED IN OUR SERVICES?
Clients we serve share several common objectives:

- They desire more top-line revenue at a faster pace.

- They may have a sales process, either homegrown, or one of the popular sales training programs. Or they are considering building a new process.

- They desire shorter sales cycles and a reduction in sales expense.

- They want their producers communicating their value propositions more clearly, in less time, when in the presence of senior level executives.

- They employ accomplished professionals who have been exposed to various sales methodologies throughout their careers.

- They believe that if their business developers are able to have an audience with one or two senior-level people in the initial meeting, they could increase their closing ratio and drive opportunities to closure more rapidly.

- They want their people presenting value propositions to an audience with more authority to make decisions, providing the opportunity to scope and assess the potential earlier in the courting cycle.

If your organization shares similar objectives, we can provide genuine benefit.

EXECUTIVE OVERVIEW

*ACCELERANT IS A RESPECTED THOUGHT LEADER IN ENTERPRISE REV-*enue acceleration, compression of sales and closing cycles, and margin enhancement. The company works with senior management, sales, business development, and marketing organizations of multinational, midsized, and small organizations—both public and private.

As a provider of business process improvement services focused on the front end of a company's business development efforts, Accelerant helps successful companies meet and exceed their numbers through strategic consulting, assessment, executive workshops, training programs, and managed services.

Our practice is focused around teaching, coaching, shaping, and helping implement field-proven business processes and repeatable methodologies that enable companies to accelerate their revenue base, compress closing cycles by up to 25 percent, reduce cost of sales levels by up to 25 percent, and reenergize senior management and field organizations with principles they enjoy using because they can produce results.

Accelerant offers organizations a cohesive set of Accelerant Principles, each uniquely connected to targeting, accessing, qualifying, and closing business opportunities in a shorter time horizon. Each principle is a skill set; its own "point solution"—allowing clients the flexibility to focus on those principles that best fit their budget and immediate needs. To view a complete listing of workshops, training programs, consulting, and managed services offerings, please visit our web site at www.accelerantinternational.com and click on Core Offerings.

CONVERSATIONS WITH THE AUTHOR

YOU CAN JOIN THE WEEKLY, BIMONTHLY, OR MONTHLY CONVERSATIONS with the author, where he discusses the constraints in greater detail, explaining how they can impede your efforts. He then highlights one Accelerant each month, discussing various applications of how they can be used to provide additional value, and taking your questions on how to utilize these tools in the field. Learn more about this opportunity by visiting the Web site.

KEYNOTE SPEAKING FOR YOUR NEXT MEETING OR COMPANY EVENT

*M*ICHAEL A. BOYLAN IS FOUNDER OF ACCELERANT, CREATOR OF THE Accelerant Principles and Accelerant Process for Business, and author of *Accelerants*. He has delivered keynote addresses for some of the most respected corporations in the United States and abroad.

Boylan is one of the highest-rated main platform speakers at the Microsoft World Fusion annual conventions. He has impressed large assemblies of several thousand people as well as small groups of senior executives in retreatlike settings. His respectful style engages audiences, creating highly interactive, humorous, and thought-provoking addresses and sessions that receive consistently high marks from the client and the audience in attendance.

For a partial list of corporations Boylan has addressed, and information on keynote fees and availability, please visit our Web site at www.accelerantinternational.com and click on Keynote Speaking.

You are also invited to call our office in Minneapolis at 952-445-7854. We can schedule a conference call to learn your particular event's goals and objectives so that we may offer suggestions about how to ensure its success.

Thank you. We look forward to being of value in the near term.

Our very best,
Accelerant

THE ACCELERANT PRINCIPLES

FIRST ACCELERANT———*ASSESS YOUR STATUS*™
SECOND ACCELERANT———*DESIGN YOUR FUTURE*™
THIRD ACCELERANT———*CHARTER YOUR COURSE*™
FOURTH ACCELERANT———*METRIC THE MESSAGE*™
FIFTH ACCELERANT———*ACCESS THE CASTLE*™
SIXTH ACCELERANT———*DELIVER THE ULTIMATE PRESENTATION*™
SEVENTH ACCELERANT———*PAINT THE FINANCIAL PICTURE*™
EIGHTH ACCELERANT———*HOLD YOUR GROUND*™
NINTH ACCELERANT———*CONDUCT THE CONCERT*™
TENTH ACCELERANT———*HARMONIZE FOR GOLD*™
ELEVENTH ACCELERANT———*CALIBRATE FOR SUCCESS*™
TWELFTH ACCELERANT———*COMPLETE THE CIRCLE OF INTEGRATION*™

INDEX